MORTAL SIN ON MY SOUL

MARY MURRAY BOSROCK

BEAVER'S
POND
PRESS

Edited by Lily Coyle and Laurie Flanigan Hegge

> *Too-Ra-Loo-Ra-Loo-Ral (That's an Irish Lullaby)* by James Royce Shannon in 1914.

> *Old Black Joe* by Stephen Foster; published by Firth, Pond & Co. of New York in 1853.

> *Queen of the May* by Mary E. Walsh in1883. Based on traditional 13th Century Catholic hymn.

> Excerpt of "The Friar's Tale" from *The Canterbury Tales* by Geoffrey Chaucer.

> Excerpt of Act 2 Scene 2 from *Hamlet* by William Shakespeare.

ISBN 13: 978-1-59298-998-0

Library of Congress Catalog Number: 2013946449

Printed in the United States of America
First Printing: 2013
17 16 15 14 13   5 4 3 2 1

Cover and interior design by James Monroe Design, LLC.

BEAVER'S
POND
PRESS

Beaver's Pond Press, Inc.
7108 Ohms Lane
Edina, MN 55439–2129
(952) 829-8818
www.BeaversPondPress.com

To order, visit www.BeaversPondBooks.com
or call (800) 901-3480. Reseller discounts available.

ALSO BY MARY MURRAY BOSROCK

Put Your Best Foot Forward Europe

Put Your Best Foot Forward Asia

Put Your Best Foot Forward Mexico/Canada

Put Your Best Foot Forward South America

Put Your Best Foot Forward USA

European Business Customs and Manners

Asian Business Customs and Manners

I Saw God

Grandma Has Wings

Dad and Mom
Thanks for giving me a home not
just to grow up in but to carry in
my heart forever.

Aunt Sabina
Thanks for loving me so much.

Mortal Sin On My Soul is a memoir.
It is the story of my life as I remember it.
Several names have been changed
to protect the marvelous!

Thanks most of all to my husband,
Ron, who has loved and supported
all my dreams for forty-seven years.
This book is being published because
of his generous heart.

CONTENTS

PART I: THE BEGINNING • 1946–1959

PART II: THE MIDDLE • 1959–1966

CONTENTS

PART III: THE END • 1966–1974

PART I
The Beginning
1946–1959

BABY BOOMER ARRIVES

JANUARY 1946

We are all born into a story that begins long before our arrival. My chapter opens in Sandusky, Ohio, January, 1946. Tommy, the firstborn and my oldest brother, spotted our family car coming down Madison Street. "The Japs are coming, the Japs are coming!" he screamed at the top of his lungs. My other five siblings, scared to death, dove under the snowy shrubs to take cover.

As Dad pulled into the driveway, Tommy calmly walked up to the car, opened the door, and had the privilege of being the first to hug Mom, finally home from the hospital. He barely glanced at me, the new baby in her arms. He was not interested or impressed. Babies were not special to Tommy. One had arrived almost every year since he was born.

On that winter day, all six Murray kids had been bundled into snowsuits and sent out to play by Aunt Sabina, Dad's favorite sister, and Jean Dovekie, our best babysitter. Aunt Sabina and Jean were hoping Mom could have a quiet moment upon her return home from the hospital, but there was no such thing as a quiet moment at 124 East Madison Street. I'd arrived into a story full of action and passion, and loaded with surprises. The larger world was about to change dramatically, as well.

The Second World War had ended and the Cold War was about to begin. For the first time in history, an atomic bomb had been used against an enemy, and the United States had used it. The soldiers were all returning from the war, buying homes, and making babies, lots of them—lots of us. We were called baby boomers, and we were about to change America.

I was number seven in the Murray family, and while no one knew it that day, there would be no more annual babies coming to 124 East Madison Street. Both the war machine and the baby machine had stopped, at least temporarily.

A Murray Christmas

It was a week before Christmas, 1948, when out of the blue, Dad jumped up from the dinner table and dashed toward the back door shouting, "I think I heard some noises outside—don't move! Did anyone else hear it? Sounded like sleigh bells to me."

The seven of us were at the kitchen table and dinner was almost finished. We were waiting for dessert. Mom had bought cookies shaped like snowmen, bells, and Santa Claus. They were frosted with a thick layer of white buttercream and decorated with red, green, and yellow sugar. The bakery truck that stopped at our house twice a week only had these cookies the few weeks before Christmas, and we loved them.

Suddenly, we were distracted from our cookie anticipation by a bell ringing outside our house. (It sounded a lot like our dinner bell.) The ringing came first from the front and then from the back of our house. We jumped up and down in our seats, screaming with excitement.

Out of breath, Dad came running back into the kitchen and sat down at the table. All seven kids were shouting: "We heard bells, Daddy. They sounded just like Santa's sleigh. We all heard it, didn't we, Mom? I know it was Santa!"

Dad acted like he hadn't heard a thing, but did suggest, "Oh, I wouldn't be surprised if the old boy was checking up on you children. Who here has been naughty, and who has been nice? What do you think, Mommy? How about Maureen? Have you been drinking your milk? Or Joe, have you been a good boy?"

Joe looked very serious as he said, "I have been really good, Daddy. I'm even trying not to wet my bed. Santa will know I'm trying, won't he?"

I was sitting next to Joe in my highchair. Joe touched my hand protectively and said, "My baby sister has been really good, too. Mary never cries." Then Joe's big eyes widened, and in an even more concerned tone he said, "Daddy, I think we should send Santa a letter telling him about Mary's problem. If he hears her crying at night, he may think she is being naughty. We need to tell him it is just Mom squirting that soapy water up her butt. It hurts. She can't help crying." (In 1948 babies whose bowels didn't move daily were given enemas. Mine didn't.)

Dad reassured him, "Oh Joe, don't worry. That ol' white-whiskered guy is pretty darn smart. He knows who's naughty and who's nice. Our sweet baby Mary is never a bad girl. Now, maybe Maureen could have a little trouble if the ol' boy sees her full glass of milk. But I'm sure she'll drink every drop tonight. Won't you, Ennie?"

Dad jumped up from the table and announced, "I think I'd better investigate this bell ringing. I'll look around the yard and see if there are any reindeer tracks in the snow."

Dashing around to the backyard and down the basement stairs, he jumped into a Santa suit at "T. J. Murray speed." Out the back door he went, grabbing the empty milk cartons that Mr. Fitz, the milkman, had left at our door. These made a perfect platform for Dad to stand on.

The older kids knew the routine, but they were delighted watching Maureen, Joe, and me with our wide-eyed belief. Pat sat quietly enjoying his new status as "wise about Santa." But the older boys couldn't miss the chance to add to Joe's misery. Since Dad was gone and Mom was deaf, they had free rein. Under his breath, Jim cackled, "Ha, ha, ha. Wonder if Santa Claus knows you are Joe the Jap. He'll think you love the Japs. You know what that will do for your Christmas haul? Flat zero—nothing but a big lump of coal. As a matter of fact, your whole stocking will probably be stuffed with coal. Ha, ha, ha."

Not wanting to be upstaged by Jim, Bob added, "Oh Joe, if Santa finds out you're Joe the Jew, he won't bring you anything— not one single present. Jewish children don't get Christmas gifts."

Tommy was enjoying the banter, but knew when it was time to end it. He said, "Okay, enough. Stop it."

Suddenly there he was. Santa Claus himself was looking into the big window in our kitchen. Bells were ringing as Santa shouted, "Ho, ho, ho!" The noise was deafening. Santa kept appearing and disappearing like a jack-in-the-box. Just when we would start to calm down, he would pop up in the window again. Each appearance caused more screams and cheers. Every time he caught sight of him, Joe yelled, "Santa, I want a raccoon hat and an atom bomb ring."

At the height of the excitement, we heard a single "Ho!" and then a loud crashing sound, followed by, "Goddammit. Son of a bitch!" And Santa was gone for good.

It was too much for my two-year-old self. I started to cry. Joe held my hand and kept saying, "It's okay, Mary. Don't cry. Santa won't bring you presents if he hears you crying."

A few minutes later, the front door opened and Dad appeared dressed as before. But now his lip was bleeding.

Mom quietly got up from the table and got Dad a warm washcloth. "Sit down, dear," she said. "We were just about to have our Christmas cookies. I'll make you some tea. It's too bad you missed Santa Claus. He was right here in our backyard. We all saw him, didn't we?"

"Sure enough, the old boy was out there," Dad told us. "I tried to catch him but he was too fast for me. He was back in his sleigh before I got to him. I slipped on that damn ice in the driveway just as the reindeer flew back up into the sky. He was checking up on us, watching to see who is good in this house. Now eat your cookies."

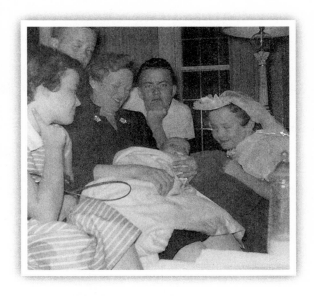

SILENT NIGHTS

Nights at our house were amazingly active. The seven of us shared three bedrooms, one bathroom, and two Wee Alert machines. The nighttime adventures varied by season, but there was never a silent night at 124 East Madison.

When Dad's size nine feet hit the ground, it was like an earthquake. Anyone in his path needed to duck and run.

Dad struggled to reach 5' 6" but he had a giant attitude. He was confident he knew how everything should be done. According to Dad, every problem had a simple solution if you just took time to think about it. "Thinkers, thinkers, thinkers—there are too few thinkers in our world," was one of Dad's all-too frequent comments.

Dad believed kids should be "housebroken" by no older than one-and-a-half years of age—which in our house meant before the next baby arrived. The fact that he had two chronic bed wetters old enough to read and write did not go over well with him.

Dad came home one evening with two huge boxes. He proudly told Mom, "Peggy, I've found the perfect solution to our bed-wetting problem. Wait until you see. These will work wonders. In no time, both Bob and Joe will be cured." With that, he pulled out the two Wee Alert machines. Dad, trying to contain his excitement, said, "You place this wired metal plate under the sheet on the child's mattress. They'll never even know it's there. But if even one drop of urine hits the metal plate, a bright red light starts flashing and an alarm warning rings."

And sure enough, when the red lights flashed and the five-alarm warning blasted through the house with less than a half-second delay, Dad would leap out of bed and his short legs would run into the dead-asleep child's bedroom. Grabbing him by the back of the neck or by his pajamas, Dad would rush him to the toilet as the alarm continued to flash and blast.

Joe's pajamas had been worn by four older brothers and washed at least a hundred times. They were threadbare, and the top never matched the bottom. Generally you would hear "rip" as Dad dragged Joe to the toilet.

Dad wasn't solely focused on defeating bed wetting, he was also big on multitasking. Bob was flunking math, and Dad was determined that it wouldn't happen. It couldn't. Flunking a grade would've required Bob to be in the classroom with next-in-line Jim. No nun, even the most saintly, was capable of handling two Murrays in the same classroom, especially if one was Bob and the other was Jim.

So when Bob's Wee Alert went off, as it did once or twice a night, Dad would haul him from his bed while shouting "Six times nine, seven times eight, five times three" on the way to and from the toilet. Bob, who was still half asleep and three-quarters blind without his glasses, would try to give the correct answers while negotiating the toilet. He generally missed one or both, which caused Dad to shout more, only now he wasn't just deafeningly loud, but also angry.

The Wee Alert machine was a year-round staple, but the symphony of sounds that accompanied it depended on the season.

At least one ventilator was part of our winter wonderland. Bob had severe asthma and often had trouble breathing when the weather was cold and damp, which was at least six months of the year in Sandusky. Since the Wee Alert required both plugs next to Bob's bed, an extension cord was plugged into the hall socket and a huge ventilator filled with water and Vicks was stationed on the other side of Bob's bed. It puffed and whistled like a steam engine as Bob coughed and wheezed.

Many nights found one of us with measles, mumps, chicken pox, croup, or the flu. Several nights every month someone was throwing up. And that was never done quietly. At the first sound of gagging, Dad would jump out of bed, grab the sick kid, and scream, "Hold it, goddammit." Most of the time it was too late, and sometimes it resulted in a chain reaction that had two or three of us sharing the toilet. Mom would have to get fresh sheets and blankets to remake the beds, but she was never impatient about it. I can still see her standing quietly and lovingly by the toilet. I can feel her hand holding my head gently as I vomited. Mom would help us back into a warm, clean bed. Covering us up and sweetly kissing us, she'd prepare for the next round.

Summer was no quieter, but the sounds were different. There was no flu or croup, and even Bob's asthma would abate. Sandusky summers were beastly hot and humid. To combat the heat, Dad insisted all windows and doors be left wide open, transforming our house into an open-air lunatic asylum.

Third-degree sunburns, poison ivy, and giant mosquito bites replaced the vomiting and croup. In order to prevent determined mosquitoes from buzzing around our heads at night, we sprayed our beds endlessly with DDT, which stunk up the whole house.

We all had pale, Irish skin, so an outdoor day usually meant nighttime pain and lots of Noxzema or calamine lotion.

We lived close to railroad tracks, and Sandusky seemed to be the night run for every train in Northern Ohio. Since the trains crossed many city streets, the engineer was required to blow the whistle loud and often. We also lived close to downtown. One of the favorite pastimes for bored teenagers in Sandusky was buzzing Columbus Avenue—or The Ave, as it was known. The later the hour, the more popular it became. To be considered really cool, you had to screech your brakes and rev your engine.

Then there were our neighbors who lived two doors down from us. They had loud and violent fights several nights a week. It wasn't as if we never heard fighting. It was our favorite pastime at 124—we kids fought daily. But we'd never heard Mom and Dad or any other adults fight before. Maureen and I would try endlessly to hear what the neighbors' screaming and fighting was about, with no luck. We would go onto the porch that was attached to our bedroom, and sometimes we would catch a glimpse of Willie and Dottie Plumme. It was like listening to an action-packed movie in a foreign language.

When we finally did get to sleep, the roosters Willie raised in their backyard would wake us up at sunrise as they began to crow.

This went on for years, until the night Willie pulled out a gun in a jealous rage. Attempting to escape, Dottie jumped into her car, and Willie jumped into his car. And Dad, hearing the commotion, jumped into his car. A short time later, Dad arrived home. We could see that he was upset. Fighting back tears, he said, "I was too late. Dottie headed to the police station hoping to get away. Willie was right on her bumper. When she arrived at the police station, she tried to run in, but he shot her before she got to the door." Mom, sitting at the kitchen table, calmly said, "Oh dear, where is poor Willie? Can we help him?"

Dad seemed to not be able to talk. He just stood there, trying to breathe. Finally, Dad did what he always did. He pulled his back straight and, swallowing tears, said, "Peggy, Willie, God rest his soul, shot himself. They are both dead." With that, Dad headed up to his bedroom.

And then there were the bats that for some reason chose to spend their summers in our attic. They would visit our bedrooms several hot nights a month.

Dad would jump out of bed and grab a tennis racket, a broom, or sometimes just his pajama top—anything he could get his hands on fast. "You son of a bitch. You bastard. I'll get you." At lightning speed, Dad's skinny legs would charge up and down the hall, in and out of our bedrooms, jumping on beds, stepping on kids. Dad was on the chase, and it usually took at least a half hour. The bat would swoop and disappear and reappear as if it was teasing Dad. But even if it took him a full hour, Dad always won.

The only peaceful sounds we heard were the church bells ringing at six thirty and eight o'clock every morning announcing the beginning of Mass. We could see the steeple from our second-floor bedrooms, and in the summer it sounded like the bell tower was in our attic.

Even the bells were often just the calm before the storm. Before the nuns left for the summer, they sent a serving schedule home with all the altar boys. Each boy was given several Masses to serve during the summer. There were five altar boys in our house, and because we lived so close to the church, the nuns loaded up the Murray boys with Masses. Also, Mom attended daily Mass, so the nuns knew she'd see to it that the server arrived, and on time. Mom would gently wake the designated boy or boys. She was proud to have her sons serving God. But if Bob or Jim were scheduled, they always tried to get out of it, which would then require the full T. J. Murray attack.

Dad slept with one eye and both ears open, always. His bed was pushed right next to the window that opened to the front of the house. He'd leave the window open so he could hear any sound from the street or the sidewalk in front of our home. He was especially interested in any neighbor who might be taking their dog for an early walk. Dad had two signs made for the yard that read, "Dogs keep off." If and when a dog got close to Murray grass, we'd hear, "Son of a bitch, that dog better not drop a load on my yard." Dad would then grab his robe and dash down the stairs and out the front door to confront the potential offenders. This was usually before 6:00 a.m.

But there was one wonderful sound that I was sure came straight from heaven. When any one of us was in need of special loving, you could hear Mom in her bedroom, comforting the child as she sang:

> *Too-ra-loo-ra-loo-ral, Too-ra-loo-ra-li,*
> *Too-ra-loo-ra-loo-ral, hush now, don't you cry!*
> *Too-ra-loo-ra-loo-ral, Too-ra-loo-ra-li,*
> *Too-ra-loo-ra-loo-ral, that's an Irish lullaby.*

On a few occasions, Dad would rock one of his children, and he always sang the same song. Not well, but with so much heart:

> *Gone are the days when my heart was young and gay,*
> *Gone are my friends from the cotton fields away,*
> *Gone from the earth to a better land I know*
> *I hear those gentle voices calling Old Black Joe.*
> *I'm coming, I'm coming,*
> *for my head is bending low,*
> *I hear those gentle voices calling*
> *Old Black Joe.*

Those were the nights I'd lie awake and whisper, "Thank you, God, for sending me to 124 East Madison Street."

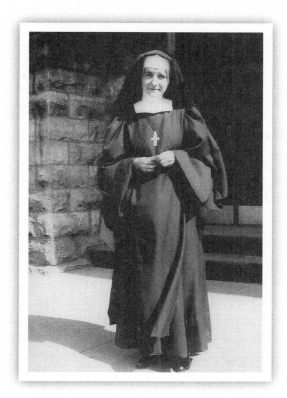

SCHOOL DAYS

It was the morning of September 7, 1951, and it was the first day of school. Our house at 124 East Madison Street was bustling.

Tom was starting eighth grade at Saint Peter and Paul, the Catholic school we all attended. Bob was starting seventh grade, Jim sixth grade, Pat fifth grade, Maureen fourth grade, and Joe third grade. I was only five, so I was to have Mom and the house to myself for the whole year. I sat in my silky blue nightgown at the back of the booth that surrounded our kitchen table, watching everyone excitedly prepare to head out and listening to their theories about which nuns would be teaching which class. Suspense on this point was high. Nuns, the Queens of Mystery, never offered hints about such things.

Eventually the front door slammed. Bang. Bang. Bang. Six times. And suddenly the house was quiet. By that time, Mom, in her starched housedress and apron, had already attended 6:30 a.m. Mass (as always), made breakfast for seven kids, and put a load of laundry in the washing machine.

Everyone had left before Dad came down to finally have a peaceful breakfast with his wife. I think it was the first time I had seen him look relaxed since school had ended last June. Even his voice sounded different this morning. "Morning, Peggy. I don't have to be in court until ten o'clock this morning. Sit down and have breakfast with me."

Then Dad stopped smiling, and the tone of his voice changed. He'd just noticed me sitting in the corner of the booth. "Mary, what are you doing here? Is something wrong with you? Why aren't you in school?"

Mom reminded him, "Oh, Tom, she's only five. She won't go to school until next year." I was Mom's shadow, and she seemed to savor the idea of one last year with her baby at home.

"What do you mean, next year? That's crazy. Who made up that rule? Mary, go upstairs and get dressed. You're going to school right now."

Mom gently protested, but I was out of there and up those steps in a flash. I was delighted to be going with the big kids. After I dressed in my favorite hand-me-down dress and Sunday shoes, I ran down the steps and out the front door to Dad's car. He was already in the driver's seat with the motor running. The school was only a block away, but Dad always drove everywhere—fast.

There was no time to be nervous. Less than a minute later, I was at school. Dad, holding my hand, walked me up the stairs. He stopped an older boy in the hall and said, "Tell me, young man, where is the first-grade classroom?"

It turned out we were right in front of it. Dad knocked on the classroom door as if he owned the place. Sister Lorraine, a petite, long-faced nun, opened the door. "Good morning, Mr. Murray. What can I do for you?" Sister Lorraine knew our family very well. She had taught, terrified, and been terrorized by all my siblings.

"Well, Sister, my pretty little baby girl, Mary Catherine, wants to start school with her brothers and sister. She is only five, but she's so smart. Show Sister, sweetie. Count to five."

"1, 2, 3, 4, 5," I said dutifully.

Sister Lorraine offered a slight smile and said, "Of course, Mr. Murray, we would love to have Mary Catherine in our class. Come in, Mary, and say goodbye to your father."

As the door closed behind me, the smile on Sister Lorraine's face disappeared. She was clearly not happy to have another student added to the forty-six already on her first-grade roster—and certainly not another Murray. To further compound the problem, Dad had unknowingly uttered the two worst words in a nun's vocabulary: pretty and smart. These two words would condemn me to classroom hell for as long as Sister Lorraine taught me. Any nun who heard *pretty* or *smart* knew they had a little sinner in the making. Their mission, as designated by God Himself, was to crack the pride and arrogance out of me. A haughty attitude, thinking you were better than others, conceit, and self-importance were all serious sins. Humility, humbleness, and meekness were virtues to be cultivated—or, if necessary, beaten into you. Either way, you would learn them. And five was not too young to start.

The classroom was full, and there wasn't a spare desk for me. Sister took me to the back of the room and grabbed a disheveled boy out of his desk. Glaring at us both she said, "Jimmy, this is Mary Murray. She will share your desk until we find a desk for her. Both of you sit down. Jimmy, share your pencils with her until she gets her own."

As Jimmy shyly handed me a pencil, I looked down at his hands.

He had no fingernails that I could see. They looked like he had chewed them down to his knuckles. Then he turned his hands over, and I could see that both of his palms were covered with huge, sore-looking warts. Sister stared at me. She said, "Jimmy will be your partner from now on. You will hold hands and walk with him, in line, to and from the playground."

I liked Jimmy, and his warts didn't bother me one bit. Sister didn't know I had spent most days during the past three months making mud pies in my backyard and decorating them with worms. There wasn't a blade of grass in that yard. It was just dirt, which was far superior to sand for making mud pies. I held Jimmy's hand in line, and later that day I walked home with him. He lived only a block from our house.

Jimmy's family was poor, and just like our family they had a kid in every class. The nuns made Jimmy's older brothers clean up whenever someone vomited in a classroom or in the church, which happened at least once a week. I told Mom how mean I thought that was. She said, "Well, that poor family doesn't have money to pay their tuition. This is the sisters' way of trying to make them feel accepted."

BENIGN NEGLECT

Benign neglect was the gift of being born number seven. Mom and Dad were always distracted and a bit worn out. No one paid much attention to me, regardless of what I did or didn't do.

Dad was determined that his children would all be well educated. Dad was hell-bent on every kid going to college—no exceptions—but I don't remember him ever looking at anyone's report card. One parent had to sign the back to prove they had actually seen it. In our house, it was always Mom. As we got older, some of us tried to fake our parents' signatures. Good grades or bad (and most were bad), my parents didn't seem to care too much unless Dad got a call from the nuns.

Calls from the nuns were frequent, and if they were made to Dad's office, they inspired extra energy. All hell would break loose when Dad hit that front door. Dad would shout, "Bob!" (or "Jim!" or "Joe!") as he was taking off his belt. The kid in question usually knew it was coming, and would have already headed up the stairs with Dad chasing on his or her heels. The bathroom door would slam and lock. Then the verbal battle would begin.

Smashing his belt against the door, Dad would yell, "Open that door, you son of a bitch, you little piece of importance!" Of course, the kid, now safely ensconced in the bathroom, would never open the door. Dad would say, "Sister Francis Regis called and said she caught you and Denny smoking during lunch behind the Methodist Church. Is that true? Open this damn door right now!"

Sometimes the bathroom inmate would offer a defense. "No, I was just talking with Denny. He was smoking, not me. Honest." This never worked.

"Okay, I'm going to get my hammer and screwdriver. Come out this minute or I'm going to take this door off." But we all knew the hinges were on the inside. Then Dad would threaten to get a ladder and come in through the bathroom window. He'd continue smashing, crashing, and banging his belt against the wall for what seemed like a lifetime. I don't remember any kid ever coming out. If necessary, they camped out in there half the night. Eventually, Dad would wear out, and the offender would sneak out of the bathroom and hide in a more comfortable place.

★ ★ ★

In the 1950s, there were no such things as learning disabilities, dyslexia, or attention-deficit disorders. No one was math-challenged. You were just smart, average, or dumb. Period. Your level of intelligence was mostly determined by your reading ability.

I was the only girl in my class in the dumb group. It should have been devastating to my self-esteem.

In my first few years of school, the nuns said I lacked application and was inattentive. I didn't know what those words meant, but I didn't think they sounded too bad. A few of my siblings were lumped in the same category, and a couple of them were considered to be worse than me, and also poorly behaved.

I was a year younger than everyone else in my class, and I hadn't attended kindergarten. No one seemed to think this was a problem. But I did everything wrong. I cut with scissors in a very convoluted fashion. Sister Lorraine cured that; she cracked my hand with a ruler until I cut correctly.

The first thing we all needed to learn was how to write our names and the initials J.M.J., which stood for Jesus, Mary, and Joseph.

Both of these were to be written on the top right-hand corner of all of our worksheets.

The J.M.J. wasn't too hard, but I struggled with my name. Sister said I needed to write my name one hundred times, until I got it correct every time.

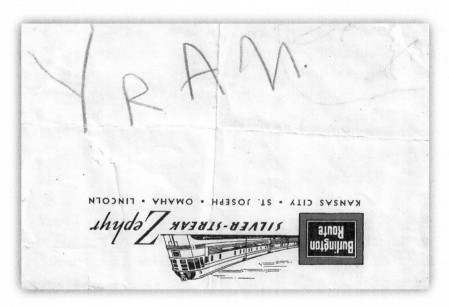

After school, I headed for Aunt Sabina's house. I told her I needed to practice writing my name. She handed me a pencil and a piece of paper. Aunt Sabina didn't even tell me I had written it backwards. And she didn't seem the least bit alarmed. She just hugged me and said, "Oh, sweetheart, you are such a smart little girl."

Maybe writing backwards with the paper upside down should have shed some light on my reading issues, but it didn't.

Sister Lorraine was better qualified to be a drill sergeant in the Marine Corps than a first-grade teacher. She had special tortures for anyone who talked in class, didn't do their homework, or did sloppy work. I mastered all three. Sister would yank me out of my desk by my ear and say, "Mary Murray, go up and down one hundred times." That's nun-speak for deep knee bends. She had eyes in the back of her head. If you didn't go all the way down each time, you had to start over. I could only count to five, so I never knew when to stop.

Even though I loved books and reading, I never could get out of the dumb "blackbird" reading group. I loved looking at the pictures and making up stories, but words were always hard for me.

All the other girls were either "bluebirds" or "cardinals." Aunt Sabina was determined to help me read better. After dinner every night, I headed across the lawn to her apartment with my reading book. With her help, I'd read the next day's story over and over until I had it memorized.

The blackbird reading group had twenty students—nineteen boys, and me. Everyone read pathetically slowly, so there was never time for more than two or three students to read aloud. When I got my chance, I was always so nervous that I read too fast and made lots of mistakes. No matter how hard I tried or how many books I memorized, I couldn't get out of the slow group. I was doomed to be a blackbird forever.

AUNTS AND UNCLES

Dad's sister, my Aunt Sabina, would never tell anyone her age, but she looked much older than Mom. She was flat chested and her over-permed hair was brown, but with a lot of white. She pulled it back from her face with a comb at each temple. Her demeanor shouted, "Sabina Isabel Murray is a no-fuss, intelligent, and capable woman!" But she was a different person with me—warm and motherly.

Our love affair began while Mom and I were still in the hospital after my birth. Dad had brought my six siblings and Aunt Sabina to the hospital to wave at Mom from the street. They had made signs: "Hi, Mom!" "Hi, Mary!" "We love you, Mom!" Mom stood in the window and held me up for all to see. They all waved and cheered. No children were allowed in the hospital, but Aunt Sabina jumped out of the car and ran in. She wanted a peek at the new baby.

By this time, Aunt Sabina was forty-six years old, and she knew she'd never have her own baby. When she saw my chubby cheeks and curly dark hair, I became her baby. From that moment, I had her unconditional love.

Aunt Sabina owned almost nothing, but she cherished what she had. One of her most cherished possessions was a hankie collection that she stored in a twelve-by-twelve leather box with a fabulous floral design on the lid. On cold or rainy days, she would take it out of the top drawer of her dresser and say, "Toots, let's look at my hankies." When she opened the box, the sweet smell of violets from a gold-beaded sachet rose from what looked like a hundred hankies. Aunt Sabina knew the story of each hankie. There were hankies embroidered with hats and hatboxes, daisies, violets, ballerinas, and birds. There were a couple embroidered with violins. (Aunt Sabina loved violin music.) Some were made in Switzerland, and some were Irish linen with lace trim. My favorite one was trimmed in red crochet with two delicate hearts in the middle. Aunt Sabina would take that one out of the box very carefully. She would look at that hankie and tell me with a wink, "Oh, I had a beau or two in my days." Then she'd close the box and give me a big hug. "Someday these hankies will all be yours, Mary."

She also had an Indian penny collection in a glass jar. Aunt Sabina seemed to like the jar more than she liked the pennies. She would look at that jar fondly and say, "This was the jar your grandfather used to fill with his famous hemorrhoid cream. He made it in our basement. People from all over would come to buy his cream. He had a nice little side business selling it." Grandpa Murray was dead long before I was born, but I knew he'd been a fireman. The side business was news to me.

Aunt Sabina was not just Dad's older sister, but also both Dad and Mom's closest friend. A year after Dad and Mom moved into 124, Dad purchased the apartment building next to our house. Mom was expecting child number four, Pat. Dad and Sabina's parents, Thomas and Rose (Rafferty) Murray had died, and the family home had been sold. The two oldest girls in the Murray family, Gertrude (Sister Francelia) and Mary (Sister Jerome), had entered the convent and become Humility of Mary nuns. This required them to close the door on their past life. They were to follow the rules of the order, and dedicate their lives to Christ. They were only allowed to write a few letters a year to their family, and visit once every four years. So Aunt Sabina, whom Dad called Red because she had red hair when she was young, had been the last one left at home. Her brothers, Emmett and Tom (my dad), were expected to get educated and earn money. The care of their baby sister, Ann, their mentally unstable sister, Lucille, and their aging parents was left to Sabina. She had never married, though Dad always said, "Red had lots of offers. She was just way too smart for them all."

Sabina worked hard at a poorly paid and thankless job (which she hated) at the Hinde & Dauch Paper Company. She called the place "Stinky Dinks." "Poor Red," my dad would say. "She does twice the work of any man in that office, and those SOBs pay her half their wages. They should be shot." She had a severe heart condition, but had to continue working to survive.

Dad gave her the nicest apartment of the four in the building. Her apartment was on the second floor, and it looked like a dollhouse. It had one good-sized room with a kitchen and dining room together. You stepped down into the only bedroom. It was tiny, but had lots of windows and was furnished with items from her parents' home on Monroe Street. I loved her apartment, and dreamed that I would live there when I grew up.

Aunt Sabina was crestfallen when she had to give up her apartment. She told Dad, fighting back tears, "The doctor said no more steps. They're too risky for my ticker."

Dad immediately prepared the ground-level apartment for her. While this apartment lacked the charm of the second-floor apartment, it brought my best pal much closer to me.

★ ★ ★

I had only one real uncle—Uncle Emmett. There was Uncle Bob, but we all knew he wasn't our real uncle. He had married Aunt Ann, the baby in Dad's family, and they lived in Beloit, Wisconsin. No one ever said anything bad about him, but we all knew Aunt Ann had married a man with a fatal flaw. He wasn't Catholic.

Uncle Emmett was Dad's big brother, and when Dad spoke about him, he made him sound like God. Unlike Dad, Uncle Emmett and his wife, Aunt Florence, went to church every day. Just like Dad, he moved at lightning speed and jangled the change in this pocket as he rushed everywhere.

One night, Dad came in from work and, dashing agitatedly into the kitchen, said to Mom, "Son of a bitch. That horse's ass Emmett doesn't know how to drive a car. They should take his license away." Mom calmly said, "Oh dear, Tom, did Emmett have an accident?" Dad said, "Accident! Accident my ass! Come out front and take a look at my car."

The house went into duck-and-run mode. Dad dragged Mom out the front door and down the steps to the end of the driveway. Joe and I followed. The rear end of Dad's beloved two-tone Ford was smashed in. Mom, looking puzzled, said, "Oh dear, you had the accident, not Emmett?"

Dad shouted, "Hell no, there was no accident. Emmett had his head up his ass. It was his fault. We were leaving the office at the same time. I jumped in my car and put it in reverse and at the exact moment, that horse's ass put his in reverse too. He smashed right into my car."

"You look alright. That's all that counts. I hope Emmett wasn't hurt."

Dad said, "Oh, he's alright. He's fine. But he shouldn't be

allowed to drive a car." From that day until the two of them went to their graves, this became the no-fault accident or the his-fault accident, depending upon who was telling the story.

Dad was seven years younger than Uncle Emmett. When he was a kid he had a stutter, and he wasn't focused like Emmett. Dad was a dreamer. He loved horses and music, the theater and dances. He would sneak into the movies to see Theda Bara, the femme fatale of his era. Dad wanted to join the merchant marines and see the world.

After high school, Dad attended Notre Dame, mostly because he loved Knute Rockne, the legendary football coach of the Fighting Irish. But when Dad got there, he found a group of entitled rich kids who made fun of his short stature and less-than-elegant wardrobe. He stayed through the football season working as a water boy for Rockne's team. Then he decided to head to California to join the merchant marines. He'd make a little money and see the world. He always loved adventure.

However, before he got to California, he stopped in Arizona and fell in love with the area. He was touring around when he spotted a group of young people who looked like his kind of guys and girls. They were all waiting to register at the University of Arizona. Dad got in line, and again became a student.

Uncle Emmett was already working for a Sandusky law firm as a bill collector. Being smart and ambitious, Emmett realized immediately that it was the lawyers who were making all the money, not the bill collectors. One day, he approached Mr. Miller, a senior partner in the law firm, and asked his advice. "I'd like to become a lawyer. Could you give me some advice on how to achieve my goal?"

Sliding his chair back and putting his feet up on the desk, Miller laughingly said, "My boy, don't let your ambition run away with you. You are a smart guy and a great worker. You will have a good future here in our office, but not as a lawyer, as our top bill collector."

Uncle Emmett said he didn't want to spend his life collecting bills; he wanted to become a lawyer.

Chuckling again, Miller replied, "Your success will come from knowing who you are and where you belong, young man. The bar isn't friendly to micks or mackerel snappers, my boy. Keep your nose to the grindstone and you will have a great future right here in our office."

Uncle Emmett left Miller's office and immediately made plans for his future. He worked every day collecting bills for the law firm, and four evenings a week he drove to Cleveland and attended evening law school classes. Two years later, he sat for the bar exam and passed. The next week, he handed Mr. Miller his letter of resignation and rented an office on the second floor above a store on Market Street. He hung a sign outside that read Emmett Murray, Attorney at Law.

Emmett knew who his clients would be, the underdog and the common man. While the well-to-do Protestant lawyers closed their offices every Wednesday at noon to spend their afternoon at the country club golfing with their clients, Emmett kept his office open. He welcomed Blacks, Poles, Italians, and Jews. Anyone who needed legal help was welcome. Sometimes he got paid, and sometimes he didn't.

After a year of working day and night in his new firm, he called Dad at the University of Arizona and told him, "I registered you at the University of Cincinnati Law School. Get back here and get your law degree. I need your help."

Two years later, Dad joined Uncle Emmett and they became Murray and Murray Attorneys at Law. The two brothers worked together until the day Dad died.

★ ★ ★

It was 1952 and the Korean War was raging. President Truman was so unpopular he had decided not to run for reelection. Fear of communism, fueled by Joe McCarthy, was sweeping the country.

I was only six years old and about to begin the second grade. We had no television, so all I knew about any of this was what I heard at home or at school. My world began and ended within a few blocks of 124 East Madison Street.

And my world (and every other kid's world in the summer of 1952) was boring. We were all supposed to stay very close to home. No swimming at pools, no going to movies, and worst of all, no

Cedar Point, our beloved amusement park. We all lived to go to Cedar Point. This summer it was off limits because of the mysterious virus called polio.

The virus's official name was infantile paralysis, because it mostly attacked children. By that summer, the number of people infected by the virus in America had soared to 58,000.

We were all herded into the gym at school to watch a grainy black-and-white movie about polio. It was worse than any horror film. There were endless stories showing children trying to walk with crutches and big metal braces on their legs. Even worse were the rows and rows of massive iron lung machines. All you could see was the head of a person who looked like they had been swallowed by the metal drum. They were all lying on their backs, looking at a mirror suspended from the machine. The orator would ask them questions. You could barely hear their answers. In a stern voice the moderator would say, "Many of these men, women, and children will be confined to these machines for the rest of their lives." We heard stories about people gagging on their vomit because they couldn't pick their heads up. There were power outages in sanitariums that housed hundreds of people who depended upon iron lungs to breathe. These stories were worse than the boogieman on my bedroom porch and my sister's stories combined. I was scared to death.

The problem was, no one knew for sure how a person got polio, or how it spread. We were told to avoid public places—especially swimming pools and movie theaters—to never swim in cold water, and to stay away from anyone with flu-like symptoms. Even without TV in our home, we were terrorized.

So 124 was a safe place (at least for our bodies). But as for our family relations, we were all spending way too much time together. We looked for anything to take us away from this horrible, forever nothingness, and from Dad, who was always finding jobs for the boys to do.

One warm Saturday morning, I awoke to the sound of Dad's voice.

"Get down here Bob, Jim, Pat—and fast," Dad shouted as he opened the front door.

Not one brother appeared. Pat was at church serving Mass. Jim, as always, managed to disappear. I was still in my nightgown, but ran into the boys' bedroom to look out the window. I knew something was going on outside, and I didn't want to miss a minute of the excitement.

A truck was pulling into the half drive between our house and Aunt Sabina's apartment. The back porch of her apartment was a spitball throw away from the window. I had a front-row seat.

The truck driver had put on big gloves and was trying to move a bed, a chest of drawers, and an old beat-up vanity table off the truck.

Joe, who was too little to help much, was there in a flash. "I can do it, Dad. Let me help." Dad said, "Get the doors, Joe. And stay the hell out of the way."

After more screaming Bob finally appeared, and Dad grabbed Pat as he arrived home from church. Jim, having heard the four-letter word "work," had slipped out the back door.

The four of them lifted the furniture out of the truck and marched it into Aunt Sabina's house. Within a few minutes, I was shocked to see Aunt Sabina's treasured dining room table and chairs being hauled out and dumped into the truck. I thought about how often she had said, "Toots, I treasure this set. It was in my family home on Hayes Avenue as long as I can remember. Your Grandma Rose loved this table. It's so full of memories of my mom and dad and sisters and brothers. Someday, when I'm dead, this will be yours. I know you will take care of it for me, and love it too."

What was going on in Aunt Sabina's house was still a mystery to me.

I jumped into my clothes and headed for her back porch. I heard Dad shout, "Stay out of the way, Mary."

Aunt Sabina, wearing her chenille robe, popped her head out of the door and said, "Hon, better not come in now. I'll see you for dinner tonight. I have a nice rolled roast, and you can have the end piece."

The blue footstool next to Aunt Sabina's stove was my second home. I sat there every day and watched Aunt Sabina cook and bake. She would make me Limburger cheese sandwiches with salt, pepper, and onions on rye bread. She always gave me tastes of everything while she talked about her life and told me stories.

At dinnertime, I headed across the lawn and could smell the aroma of beef and onions. Aunt Sabina always stuffed chopped onions into little pockets she carefully cut in the meat. She would salt and pepper the meat before roasting. As it roasted, it smelled like nothing else on earth. Aunt Sabina would pull the roast out of the oven about thirty minutes before it was finished. She would slice off the end piece and give it to me. The taste of the medium-rare beef and salted onions melted on my tongue. To this day, I have never tasted anything better. Of course it was dished up with the aroma of unconditional love.

"Hi, Aunt Sabina," I yelled as I opened the back door. As always, Aunt Sabina gave me a big hug, but I immediately noticed the kitchen was different. The table was set for three people. Her kitchen and table were so small there was barely room for two. Now my footstool was seated at the table with two other chairs.

Suddenly, a heavyset lady wearing a paisley dress appeared in the kitchen. To my astonishment, Aunt Sabina calmly said, "Mary, this is your Aunt Lucille. She is your dad's and my sister. She is going to be living here with me."

From the kitchen, I could see the bedroom furniture that had been unpacked that morning, now squeezed into Aunt Sabina's tiny dining room.

They say our ancestors are hidden in every cell of our bodies, but I never expected an actual hidden aunt to suddenly appear. Worst of all, Aunt Sabina's house was my special place in the world. This is where I came to get Black Jack gum and pink candy, and to have someone pay complete attention to me. This stranger was now going to occupy my beloved little space and share my Aunt Sabina. My territory was being invaded, and I wasn't thrilled to find out I had a new relative.

Aunt Lucille was the largest woman I had ever seen. She was average height, but very fat. This was unusual for my family. All the women and men were trim.

But this night at Aunt Sabina's house, I learned a lot about my new family member, Aunt Lucille.

First of all, while I was surprised and trying to process her existence, she was equally surprised that I existed. And she didn't know that I had five brothers and a sister, either. She was shocked that her mother, her father, and her sister Mary (Sister Jerome) were all dead.

Aunt Sabina would get annoyed every time Aunt Lucille would say, "How is Mary doing," or, "Will Mother be coming to see me soon?"

"Stop that Lucille, you know Mother is dead. She has been dead for years," Sabina would coldly reply. With that, Aunt Lucille would cover her eyes and cry, but just a little, before she returned to her plate of beef, potatoes, green beans, and Jell-O salad.

I also learned that Aunt Lucille was a kind, sweet, simple soul who wished no harm to anyone. She loved her parents, her family (at least the ones she remembered), and most of all, she loved God. Actually, God might have tied food for first place. Aunt Lucille really loved food.

Aunt Sabina put a nice plate of food in front of Aunt Lucille. But before Lucille began to eat, she reached into the pocket of her dress and pulled out a rosary. Now I knew the rosary very well. We said the family rosary every evening after dinner in the small hall outside our bedrooms.

However, I had never seen anyone do what Aunt Lucille did. She put her rosary around her plate like a little frame. She then took out a picture of the Blessed Virgin and a picture of the Sacred Heart and placed them in front of her plate.

I was only six years old, so it looked okay to me. But I could tell it annoyed Aunt Sabina to no end. She didn't say anything, but she straightened her back and glared at her sister. I had never seen her look this mean before. That look said, "This is going to be a long, difficult adjustment."

Suddenly the phone rang, and Aunt Sabina jumped up from the table and squeezed past Aunt Lucille, running down the hall and into her bedroom where the phone sat on her nightstand.

It was long distance from Aunt Sabina's baby sister who lived in Beloit, Wisconsin. "Oh, hi Ann. Good to hear your voice. Yes, yes, she arrived a few hours ago. She is okay, but way too fat. She is also smoking cigarettes. I made it clear to her she would have to go outside to smoke. With my ticker problems, the last thing I need is cigarette smoke. And of course, she would stink my place up to the high heavens."

While Aunt Sabina was out of sight and distracted, Aunt Lucille ate all her dinner and piled more food on her plate—a lot more food. She mixed together two slices of beef, mashed potatoes, green beans, and Jell-O with fruit cocktail. Her plate looked like a garbage pile. She was enjoying eating the disgusting-looking mush when Aunt Sabina returned to the table.

Aunt Lucille had a voracious appetite. I think she would have eaten the whole roast if Aunt Sabina had not angrily whisked the food off the table.

DEAFENING SILENCE

I don't remember very clearly what our home was like before that fateful Fourth of July in 1952, but I assume it was different and better. As I got older, I wished I could just go to sleep on July 3rd and wake up on July 5th.

Since the beginning of my life, Mom had always been deaf. Neither she nor anyone else in our house ever talked about her hearing problem. As a small child, I just always knew Mom had one good ear and one bad ear. We all knew that we needed to turn toward her left ear when we talked to her. She called that her "good ear."

Once I heard my mom's sister, our Aunt Sis, say something about Mom being born deaf in her right ear, but I didn't ask any questions. If someone asked bluntly about her hearing problem, Mom always laughingly said, "Isn't God wise? He gave me all these children and bum hearing. Aren't I blessed?"

Mom was not a party person, and for sure not a country club lady. She was delighted to drop us off at the Plum Brook Country

Club pool in the summer, and she knew Dad loved to play golf there, but she avoided going there if she could get out of it.

That fateful year, Plumbrook was having a Fourth of July party for adults. Dad urged her to go with him. "Mommy, let's go. It'll be fun. Mary can stay at Sabina's." I was the only one too young to stay alone. Having no excuse, Mom agreed.

The next morning when I woke up, I could feel tension hanging over the house. It was almost like the house itself was shouting "ouch." It didn't take long before I heard the story. Eddie Lentz, the funeral director who lived two doors from the church, had thrown a firecracker under Mom's chair on the patio at the country club. When it blasted off she was shocked, but worse than that, she couldn't hear. Not a sound. Everyone was running around, trying to help her but she just smiled and said, "Please don't fuss over me. I think I'd just like to go home."

Thanks to that firecracker, Mom was now completely deaf. It had broken the eardrum in her good ear. Dad was enraged. "That moron, that son of a bitch, that immature bastard, that horse's ass." Every word in Dad's repository came spilling out. "I'm going to sue that son of a bitch."

I guess the silver lining was that Mom didn't have to hear Dad's raging. She looked tired and worried but didn't say much. Dad called Dr. Killoran, our family doctor and his good friend. Dr. Killoran, trying to calm Dad, said, "Now take it easy, Tom. Sometimes this happens and after the trauma, the ear drum heals. Just give it a few days. I'll get Margaret an appointment with a great ear doctor in Toledo. He's the best in Ohio and he can evaluate her."

Eventually, Mom did regain partial hearing in her good ear— enough to survive a house full of kids. But the Fourth of July remained a black holiday at 124 East Madison Street.

FOWL AFFRONT

Dad used to announce in his loud, bombastic voice, "When T. J. Murray dies, half the town will weep and half the town will cheer, but everyone will know I am gone."

I sometimes wished for and wondered what it would be like to have a quiet, average Dad. My dream dad would wear flannel shirts and read books and smoke a pipe quietly in front of the fireplace. In my make-believe home, my dream dad might, for example, choose to ignore pigeon poop on Thanksgiving Day— especially just as his family and guests were arriving. But my home and my dad were not normal.

Thanksgiving Day 1952 was cold, so Joe and I bundled up and went outside to wait for Aunt Sis (Mom's older sister and her only sibling) to arrive from Cleveland. We were sitting on the front steps and could hardly wait. Aunt Sis was an important career woman who dressed like a big-city lady. Her skin was delicate, almost translucent. Her refinement and even her voice reflected the years she had studied at the exclusive Catholic girl's school,

Lourdes Academy. She had curly hair that she wore naturally. She smelled of lavender and wore a coat with a big fur collar, high heels, and gloves. She always wore gloves, winter and summer.

We only saw Aunt Sis on holidays, and she always arrived carrying two black tin cans adorned with pink and green flowers, filled with homemade chocolate and surprise cookies. While we loved Aunt Sis, we adored her cookies. She also brought fancy chocolate candies, pastel mints, and mixed nuts loaded with cashews. All of her offerings were purchased from Stouffers, and each box was wrapped in beautiful paper and tied with fancy velvet ribbons. Aunt Sis would ask Joe and me to help her place a six-inch white or milk chocolate turkey at each child's place at the table. Best of all, each turkey had a small envelope tied to its neck with a bright ribbon. Inside was a crisp, new ten-dollar bill.

As Joe and I waited for Aunt Sis and her rare treasures, Dad checked the cracked bricks on the front steps of the house. Dad never took a day off. He was always engaged in some attempt to control at least his corner of the world. Suddenly he saw ten or fifteen pigeons flying overhead, depositing big, white globs on the roof of our house and his apartment building next door.

Outraged at the fowl affront, Dad charged into the house. He grabbed his shotgun from the coat closet in the foyer, dropping shells all over the tile floor as he attempted to load it. We lived in a city neighborhood filled with family homes set very close to each other, which made shooting a gun very dangerous, not to mention illegal. But that didn't bother Dad one bit.

He flew out the front door in full attack mode, and our yard became a battlefield—Dad versus the pigeons. Joe and I were invisible observers.

"You son of a bitch. You won't see the light of another day after T. J. Murray deals with you!" Dad missed pigeon after pigeon. An endless array of bad words spilled out of his mouth, louder and louder with each escaped bird.

Joe jumped up to run into the kitchen where Mom, who had been up since five o'clock that morning, was finishing the last-minute preparations for a Thanksgiving feast for seventeen people: turkey, mashed potatoes and gravy, cranberry sauce, rolls, various vegetables, Jell-O, and mixed salads—not to mention homemade pies. "Mom, Mom, hurry. Come outside. Dad is committing a mortal sin on the front lawn." The mortal sin, Joe reported, wasn't killing pigeons or breaking the law—it was that Dad had said, "Son of a B and God D it."

She put her arm around Joe and said softly, "Joe, you're always my good helper. Please put ice in all the water glasses on the table. Oh, and get the pitcher out of the cupboard and fill each glass with water. Try not to spill." Mom was always trying ever so gently to bring a bit of civility to her brood. She had been reared in a genteel home, in which manners were important. The Cummings family thought of themselves as lace-curtain Irish. Surely a pigeon shoot wouldn't have been on their Thanksgiving agenda. But Mom was unfazed.

★ ★ ★

Thanksgiving was special for all of us. It was the first holiday after the start of school in September, and it launched the excitement of Christmas.

I couldn't wait to get home from school on the Wednesday before Thanksgiving. As I opened the front door, the smell of cinnamon and nutmeg coming from the apple and pumpkin pies baking in the oven permeated the house. By no later than four o'clock, the back doorbell would ring, and, as Mom would always say, "that pretty Davlin girl" would deliver a thirty-eight-pound turkey. The Davlin kids went to school with us. They owned a picture-perfect farm just outside of town. Each Thanksgiving, Christmas, and New Year's, 124 East Madison hosted the biggest turkey their farm produced.

Immediately upon the bird's arrival, Mom would take out the neck, heart, gizzard, and liver, and begin simmering them in chicken broth along with chopped onions. As they cooked, we'd get our first whiff of the next day's feast. Mom would ask Joe or me to find the long wax wicks, which required a treasure hunt in the catchall drawer next to the stove. It held foil saved for reuse, greasy hot gloves, toothpicks, string, straws, plastic bags, rubber bands, and loads of Tums, matches, and the long wax wicks. Mom would light the wick and burn the long hairs off the turkey. Joe and I would be right there, eager to help. She would then wash out the turkey and fill its cavity with towels. Too big for the refrigerator, Mom would put the turkey in the cold room just off the kitchen.

I loved helping Mom set the holiday table. We used all our best stuff—a crisply starched white Irish linen tablecloth, white linen napkins, cut glassware that was supposed to look like Waterford, Noritake china, and stainless steel utensils that were supposed to look like sterling silver. There was always a centerpiece of fresh fall colors of orange, gold, and green flowers adorning the center of the table. When Mom and I finished, the Murray dining room looked liked Buckingham Palace awaiting the Queen herself.

Dad's holiday jobs were to carve the turkey, open the wine, and cause a commotion. The last was his specialty. Mom would have Dad's apron and chef hat cleaned and ironed, and the knives were always freshly sharpened for Dad's big, noisy "carve the turkey" show. This year, just after Mom had lifted the turkey out of the oven and started scooping the dressing out of the cavity so Dad could begin to carve, we suddenly heard from the butler's pantry: "Son of a bitch. What happened to my wine? Where is that damn Bob?"

Dad's voice carried for miles and struck fear in the most courageous of hearts. He'd gone looking for the wine bottle he'd opened earlier. It was empty except for one swallow. Everyone scattered out of the kitchen, except Mom.

Bob, who was now a teenager and over six feet tall, came running into the kitchen carrying the leather-bound Bible that sat on the end table in our living room. He slammed the book on the kitchen table in front of Dad. "I swear on the Bible," Bob shouted, placing his right hand on the book. "I never touched the wine—not one drop."

Then from the far corner of the booth that surrounded our kitchen table, Dad heard a hiccup followed by a huge belch. Aunt Lucille sat there looking comfortable. Dad, with his face turning beet red, shouted, "Son of a bitch! You drank the entire bottle of wine, Lucille. You're a hog."

Thanks to that bottle of red wine and a frontal lobotomy, Lucille was untroubled by his insults. Calmly, almost cheerfully, she replied, "You are a stingy, mean old man denying your older sister a little wine on Thanksgiving Day."

"You're disgusting. A little wine, my ass. You drank the whole damn bottle. Now there's no wine for *me* to enjoy with *my* Thanksgiving dinner. Son of a bitch."

"Oh, Thomas, Thomas, Thomas," she chided. "Behold the lilies of the field, they neither toil nor sow; yet our dear Lord takes care of all their needs."

With that, Dad lost it again. This time completely. "The Lord? The *Lord*? Like hell, the Lord. Are you crazy? Do you know who takes care of you? Do you know who pays your bills, puts a roof over your head, and puts food on your table? *Not* the Lord. Your brother. Meeeee, little old Tommy Murray. Not the goddamn Lord!"

It was true. Dad not only provided housing and food for his two sisters, Sabina and Lucille, but he had also paid for Aunt Sabina's two heart operations and Aunt Lucille's frontal lobotomy and frequent stays in Toledo State Mental Institution.

★ ★ ★

Aunt Lucille would sit on the back porch of Aunt Sabina's apartment for hours, quietly staring blankly and rocking in her chair. However, when Aunt Sabina was in the house making dinner or talking on the phone, Aunt Lucille would tell me stories about her family. I had grown to enjoy listening to her. When she spoke, she articulated every word, and her face became animated. She told me all about my great-grandfather, Thomas MacMurray. "Grandpa MacMurray was a soldier in the Scottish army, and one day he had a fight with a high-ranking officer. They both drew their pistols and shot. Great-grandfather killed that officer. And when he saw his dead body, he knew he needed to flee Scotland, or he would be hung. He fled to Ireland, and changed his name to Thomas Murray."

With her eyes tearing, she said, "When I was in the hospital, my dear, dear mother, Rose, visited me often. She would sit on my bed and tell me all about Jesus and the saints. Occasionally she would bring the Blessed Mother with her. I could see her standing right by my bed, but I can't tell you what Mary looks like, because Her beauty is blinding. One night I was in the worst pain I had ever felt. My skin felt like it was on fire, and I hurt right down to my bones. That night, my mother, who had died before I went into the hospital, came to the foot of my bed and said, 'Lucille, I love you so much.' And then she disappeared."

I never told Aunt Sabina these stories because she always

seemed annoyed with Aunt Lucille. But I told my sister Maureen the stories and asked, "Do you think they are true?" Maureen said, disgusted by my stupidity, "Are you cracked, too? Why do you think Aunt Lucille is in the mental institution?" I guess that meant no.

★ ★ ★

Aunt Lucille had only been with us for one Thanksgiving. Her second Thanksgiving began with the usual holiday chaos. We were all waiting for two o'clock, the time Mom always served dinner on holidays. Aunt Sabina had arrived earlier, with her apron on, to help with the meal. Mashing the potatoes, making the gravy, and cutting the cranberry sauce into little half moons were her duties. She knew how to help without getting in the way.

When two o'clock came, there was no sign of Aunt Lucille. Aunt Sabina was annoyed and said, "Mary, hon, run next door and tell Lucille to get over here."

I didn't even put my coat on to walk the few steps to Aunt Sabina's apartment. I knocked, and as always, walked right in. "Hi, Aunt Lucille. Where are you? We're going to eat very soon."

I heard her jolly voice say, "I'm in here, dear. In my bedroom."

Aunt Lucille's bedroom was Aunt Sabina's former dining room. It held a small bed, a vanity table, and a dresser. I found Aunt Lucille lying spread-eagle on the floor, looking quite happy and content. "Oh my dear, will you be kind enough to just give me your arm? I need a bit of help to get up," she asked.

As I tried to pull all two-hundred-plus pounds of Aunt Lucille to her feet, I noticed that her leg looked like it was in two pieces. I was terrified. It looked like it was going to break off right in front of me.

"I'm sorry, Aunt Lucille. You can't get up. Your leg is broken. Are you in terrible pain?"

"Not at all, dear. I'm just fine. I don't want to miss your mother's lovely meal. If I can just get up, I'm sure I can make it."

"I'm going to get Dad. Please don't move," I said in a panic.

I ran back into our house just as Dad was finishing carving the turkey and everyone was gathering at the table. Holding back tears I called, "Dad, Aunt Sabina—come quickly. Aunt Lucille is on the floor and her leg looks like it's going to fall off."

Neither Dad nor Aunt Sabina looked happy as they headed out the door. In a minute, Dad was back. "Son of a bitch. Lucille broke her leg. Tom, Bob, Jim, and Pat get over there with me. I have to get her to the hospital." Dad and the four boys struggled, but were finally able to drag Aunt Lucille into the backseat of the car.

As Dad pulled away with Sabina and Lucille, Joe came out of the house and started running down the street after the car yelling, "Stop, Dad! Stop!" He was carrying a huge plate covered in foil. When Dad pulled over and stopped, Joe opened the back door where Aunt Lucille was sitting. "Here, Aunt Lucille," he said. "Mom didn't want you to miss your Thanksgiving dinner."

At school when someone acted crazy, we would say, "You should be in Cherry Street." We all knew that meant the Toledo State Hospital for the mentally ill. After Aunt Lucille's leg healed, she didn't return to Aunt Sabina's apartment. Her depression and hallucinations had returned, and she went directly back to Cherry Street.

DON THE DAGO

Before I was old enough to go to school, I knew three things. We were Irish, we were Catholic, and we didn't talk to our next-door neighbors.

I didn't know what Irish meant, except that it was good, and that I was lucky to be born that way. Neither of my parents had ever been to Ireland. None of my grandparents had ever been to Ireland either. But the Murrays were 100 percent Irish, and proud of it.

I knew a little more about being Catholic. I'd seen my siblings prepare for and receive First Communion and even Confirmation, in the cases of the older ones. It was the one and only true faith. Catholics went to heaven, and no one else did. So I was lucky there, too.

Also, a few of the first words I learned to say were, "Mortal sin on my soul." I said this long before I knew what mortal sin was about. My sister made Joe and me say it before she would tell us any secrets. We had to not just promise not to tell, but had to swear,

"Mortal sin on my soul."

For what seemed like an eternity, in the evenings we would kneel in the hall outside our bedrooms and say the family rosary. Mom always said, "The family that prays together, stays together." It seemed to be working—we were certainly together. Mom would allow each child to lead one decade of the rosary. Since there was no TV in our house, there wasn't much else to do. But the family rosary idea didn't last too long. The only two who really got into it were Mom and Pat. Dad never attended.

We all knelt in our upstairs hallway beneath a huge picture of Our Lady of Fatima floating above a bush with three children kneeling below her. The Blessed Virgin had appeared to these children. We weren't sure if she talked to them about other things, but we all knew she gave them three messages to tell the world. The first one was a vision of hell. The second one contained Mary's instructions on how to avoid hell and save souls by converting the world to the Catholic faith, especially Russia. The third message was a secret. The Pope had it, we knew, but had been told not to open it and tell the world until 1960. We all loved the idea of a secret, and we kept guessing what the third message was. Most of us thought it would predict the end of the world, or an atom bomb dropping on America. Waiting until 1960 for the secret to be revealed seemed impossible, but what could we do? The orders came straight from the Blessed Virgin herself.

So I'd had a little exposure to being Catholic, but I had no idea why we didn't talk to our neighbors, Mr. and Mrs. Dago.

It was hard to know a person's real name. Our mean babysitter was called Horrible Helen, and the nuns were Sister Pig Face, Sister Kraut Head, and Sister Stretch Nose. Our rich false uncle was called Uncle Buck, and his big-breasted wife was called Humpty Bumpty. Father Stein was known as Father Frank N. Stein.

My siblings had given each other names way before I was born, too. They were all baptized with nice saints' names like Thomas, Robert, James, Patrick, Maureen, and Joseph—but instead of using those names, they called each other Bully, Pig Head, Four Eyes, Pee Wee Wet Bed, Sour Grapes, Patsy Pale Face, Liver Lips, Harlequin, and Skinny Witch. Dad called all of them Mortimer Snerd, the name of the slow-witted puppet Edgar Bergen had developed for his radio and (eventually) TV program. If they acted stupid (which at least one of them did most days), they were Mortimer Snerd. Dad even called Maureen "Blondie" after Dagwood Bumstead's empty-headed wife. Clearly he didn't spend a lot of time worrying about his children's self-esteem.

But I did know that our neighbors, the Dagos, were our enemies—this was crystal clear without anyone telling me. How that had come to be was another issue. My siblings knew all kinds of secrets that had happened before I was born. No one ever discussed them. I just needed to try to figure it all out. I guessed that the Murrays were on speaking terms with the Dagos before I was born. By the time I was old enough to talk, though, not one word passed between us, not even "hello."

Our houses were close. We even shared a common driveway, not that I ever saw anyone drive a car onto it. It was the driveway to nowhere. Dad had put up a basketball net at the top of the driveway for two reasons. First, and most importantly, he wanted to establish ownership of the property. Second, basketball was a good way to keep five boys busy.

Don Dago had pitch-black hair that looked like he colored it with shoe polish. He was a small man who looked perfectly nice and normal to me. So did Jo, his wife, and his son Barry. I could see the Dagos' backyard from my bedroom window. I used to watch Mrs. Dago hanging laundry on the line while little Barry played soldiers or rode his bike. Barry had a fuzzy red-haired dog that looked more like a four-legged wig than a dog. But when I played outside in our yard, I never looked at the Dagos' yard so no one would see me looking.

I always crossed the street in front of my house just in case any of the Dagos were on their porch or in their driveway. But one day I found myself trapped. I saw Mrs. Dago walking down the street straight toward me. There was no place to hide. As she got closer, I panicked. I looked down but I knew she was getting closer and closer. Then she was right in front of me. Her eyes met mine and with my heart in my throat I said, "Hi." To my shock, Mrs. Dago smiled nicely and said, "Hello, Mary Catherine." I couldn't believe it. She knew not just my first name, but also my middle name.

It took three minutes to walk home from school, and I loved going home for lunch with Mom. One lovely spring day, Pat stopped home for lunch, too. He had served a funeral Mass at 11:00, and missed Mrs. McKenna's lunch in the cafeteria. Pat was in the seventh grade then, and I was so proud of him. He was quiet and serious, and never mean. And he was really holy. Everyone knew he was going to be a priest. That helped all the Murray children get in good with the nuns. Pat saved the rest of us from the wrath inspired by Bob and Jim, who the nuns hated for good reason.

Bob was just a poor student. Jim was a different story. Jim was smart, and probably should have been excommunicated before he even started school. He didn't buy the program, and the nuns didn't scare him. He learned quickly and spent the rest of his time figuring out how to tease other students, and most of all, how to have fun. Once I caught Jim and my cousin Denny behind the Methodist church smoking cigarettes and drinking beer during lunchtime. They bribed me with gum, and told me not to tell anyone. I didn't, but I worried, because I thought they were committing lots of mortal sins. Drinking and smoking in the eighth grade had to be a sin, I thought. But even worse, we were forbidden to even look at the Methodist or Lutheran churches that were across the street from school.

Pat finished his lunch and said, "Come on, Marzie. I'll walk you back to school." I was pleased about that, because I loved walking into school with Pat. I hoped the nuns would see me and think I was good and holy, too.

When we left, Pat didn't cross the street right away. Instead he turned left and headed toward the Dagos' house. I dropped my eyes until we passed it. Then I whispered to Pat, "Have you ever talked to any of the Dagos?"

Pat stopped so fast it scared me. He turned to me and in an angry voice said, "What did you say?"

My eyes welled up with tears. I didn't realize it was *that* bad to talk to our neighbors. Terrified, I said, "I didn't talk to them, honest. I just wondered if you ever did."

"What did you call them? Did you say *dagos*? That's a very nasty word, and I'm shocked you would talk like that. Don't ever use that word again. We don't talk to Mr. and Mrs. Bonner or Barry. Dad had a fight with them years ago. But we don't call them bad names in public either."

Bonner. That was the first time I'd heard that name. Pat didn't explain what *dago* meant, but his reaction made it clear that it was bad.

Dad prided himself in telling every person what he thought, and never behind anyone's back. "I tell the truth, and I tell it to every man, face to face." Apparently Dad had told Don Bonner something to his face before they quit talking. But I had no idea what it was.

Finally I asked Joe, "Why don't we talk to the Bonners?"

According to Joe, "It was Jim's fault. And a little bit Tom's and Bob's, too. Barry came home from the county fair, and he was so proud of the huge gas balloon his parents had bought him. He was holding onto it for dear life as he played in front of his house. Tom and Bob had just finished playing basketball. They saw Barry and told him to let the balloon go. But Barry wouldn't. He said his dad told him to never let it go or it would be gone forever. They told him if he let it go it'd circle around a cloud and come right back. And bring loads of candy with it. So Barry let it go. Of course, the balloon never returned."

"That's why we don't talk to the Bonners?" I asked.

"No, then Jim saw wet leaves and dirt that spilled out of the Bonners' gutters onto our driveway. He decided it would be fun to toss them back onto their newly painted house."

Dad had been endlessly annoyed about their gutters emptying onto the shared driveway. When Mr. Bonner called and told Dad what Jim had done, Dad asked, "How do you know it was Jim? And if you cleaned your gutters out properly it never would have happened." Jim didn't even get into trouble. But from that day on, the Murrays didn't talk to the Bonners.

★ ★ ★

Dad decided he needed to demarcate the property line between our houses. Early one Saturday morning, I heard a loud banging outside my bedroom. It sounded like metal being pounded into metal. When I looked out the window, a truck had pulled into the driveway between our house and the Bonners' house. Two men were unloading piles of rusted railroad tracks. Dad was orchestrating the placement of the track at the edge of the driveway almost on top of the Bonner's house. By noon it looked like a train might come up the drive any minute. Our driveway to nowhere now had a train track to nowhere too. Dad was happy, certain he had clearly established ownership of the driveway.

The rusted tracks looked awful. But Dad was never without a solution. "Peggy, I'll get the boys to paint those tracks white and plant flowers between the tracks," he announced at lunch. "Wouldn't pansies and daisies and maybe even a few rose bushes look great? The Bonners should be grateful. This will improve their property too."

As always, Dad had found the perfect solution.

MOM'S KITCHEN

Going into our kitchen felt like going back into Mom's womb. Every sight and smell spoke of Mom's love and comfort. Standing at the picture window above the sink, we looked out on our giant elm tree and the most amazing rope swing in America. I spent hours of my life on that swing. Once I was old enough to pump, I could go above the treetops in our neighbor's yard. And I could almost see into our second-floor bathroom.

Mom encouraged my interest in cooking. She was glad to turn the kitchen over to me after so many years of feeding endless mouths morning, noon, and night. I came home from school each day, and immediately went to the kitchen and began baking and cooking. By the time I was nine, I could easily make dinner for the entire family.

Everything, good and bad, happened in our kitchen at the tan vinyl booth that seated ten. Stomachs were filled, stories were told, games were played, newspapers were read, homework was done, tears fell, and fights broke out—lots of them. Everyone had his or her designated place.

Mom tried to make sure we were well fed. But she also attempted to create an environment of civility. At every dinner, the table was covered with a tablecloth, and each place had a knife, fork, and spoon in their proper places and a cloth—not paper—napkin. Milk was served from a pitcher. Mom never put a catsup or mustard bottle on the table. Any condiments were put in small dishes with little serving spoons and placed on the lazy susan in the center of the table.

Dad worked endlessly to teach us manners. "Take your elbows off the table. Joe, sit up straight. Put your napkin on your lap. Maureen, eat your meat and drink your milk. Jim, bring the soup up to your mouth, not your mouth down to the soup. Pat, quit that damn smacking."

Joe had a strange stomach. Certain foods—like baked beans—made him gag. We had baked beans often. Poor Joe would look at his plate, assessing his situation. Should he get sick, or incur Dad's wrath? Dad would say, "Joe, just take one bite. Everyone loves baked beans. It's all in your head."

When Joe worked up the courage to take the first mouthful, Jim would whisper, "Greasy grimy gopher guts." Joe would jump up from the table gagging and head for the bathroom. Then, if there were enough distractions, Jim would dump his baked beans onto Joe's plate.

★ ★ ★

For a few years, Dad tried to get everyone to the table by ringing five bells that were attached to a metal bar like the set on the altar at church. He got them from his friend Father Armitage. Dad knew the answer to everything, but on occasion he would ask for advice from what seemed like poorly qualified sources. Once I overheard him tell Mom, "I asked Father Armitage if he thought it was necessary to talk to the boys about the facts of life. Father said, 'Why, nobody told us. Let them learn the same way we did, in the street.'" I think Dad was relieved.

When we heard the bells from Father Armitage ringing, we were supposed to drop whatever we were doing and rush to the dinner table. It never worked.

So Dad tried another, much better, idea. "I found the perfect solution," he told Mom. Fire Chief MacGlocken was another of his friends. He asked the fire chief to get him a firehouse alarm. Dad was so proud of his new idea. He could hardly wait until he could test it at dinner that night.

Dad said, "Peggy, the alarm requires minor electrical work, just a simple deal. I asked Joe Vivano to wire it in for me." Joe owned the fruit stand a few blocks from our house. Mom stood at the sink sweetly doing the lunch dishes with a look of resignation. She had lived with Dad long enough to know nothing was ever going to be simple.

As the front doorbell rang, Dad jumped up from the table. "Okay, Peggy. Joe is here and I know the perfect place for him to hang the alarm. Right here on the steps going down to the basement. Now look, everyone will be able to hear it, but it will be out of sight, not an eyesore. Okay Joe, do your magic. Thanks. See you for dinner, Peggy." Out the door Dad flew.

I don't know what Joe Vivano's qualifications were for doing electrical work. I suspect Dad had done legal work for him. Rather than charging Joe, Dad would have him rewire the house.

Dad was so proud of his new idea. He could hardly wait until dinner. "Oh, Peggy, wait until you see how great this works. Every kid will be here in less than a minute. Even if they're in the backyard, or across the street at the Lehrer's, they'll hear it and come running."

My brother Joe and I were already standing in the hall waiting excitedly for the virgin ring. Dad pushed the button, and the DONG DONG DONG sent us all running as far as possible. Even Mom, who was already deaf, covered her ears and ran into the sunroom. Dad could not figure out how to turn it off. "Goddammit, where is that damn off button? That horse's ass! Get Joe Vivano on the phone." Apparently Mr. Vivano was better at growing fruit than wiring electrical devices. He'd almost burned our house down on his previous home repair visit.

The deafening siren could be heard for blocks. The neighbors were all coming out of their houses to see where the fire was. Someone called the fire department. Within five minutes there were two fire trucks, a half-dozen firemen, and several neighbors surrounding our house.

Dad's fire bell hung there for as long as I lived at 124 East Madison, but that day was the first and only time I ever heard it ring.

★ ★ ★

We did three things that assured us we were Irish. We laughed often, finding humor in what other people found grim. (The grimmer, the funnier, actually.) We fought whenever we got the chance, which was always. And we ate potatoes.

The Irish say only two things in this world are too serious to be jested on: potatoes and matrimony. We never saw a noodle or a grain of rice in the Murray kitchen. We ate potatoes every day. Some people had a wine cellar; we had a potato cellar. On the first Monday of every month, the potato man delivered three hundred potatoes to the bin in our basement. Every night, pan in hand, Mom would grab the nearest kid and instruct, "Go to the potato room and get ten nice, big potatoes." Then Mom would peel, boil, and mash them, adding a full stick of butter and several cups of whole milk. Occasionally, she'd scallop or bake them with chicken, in both cases covering the potatoes with ample amounts of Campbell's cream of mushroom soup.

Mom and Dad were frugal. With ten mouths to feed, plus Dad's two sisters to support, they really had little room to splurge. However, food was one area where they never conserved. They remembered the days when people died of consumption, and it left a big impression on them.

Mom recycled everything. She cleaned and reused foil and plastic bags. The stove had foil covering the drip pans. They were changed by turning the foil over twice a year. The only boy who got new clothes was Tom.

★ ★ ★

Mom and Dad had one car. Mom seldom drove anywhere except to Gundlach's grocery store every Friday night. She took Aunt Sabina and me with her. It was the highlight of my week. Mom said the same thing every Friday night before we left for the store: "Mary, don't ask for a book. They cost too much, and you have every book already." But the Golden Book display was just too tempting.

As soon as we arrived, I'd head to the bookrack. In no time, I was in love with one of them: *Bambi*, *The Fire Engine*, *The Three Little Pigs*, *Uncle Remus*, *The Spotted Puppy* . . . the selection was endless. They cost between twenty-five and thirty-nine cents. That was a lot of money, so I didn't want to ask Mom. I would go to Aunt Sabina and show her the book. She always put it in her cart.

Mom would fill her shopping cart to the brim. Often the other customers were shocked by the amount of food she gathered, and the cost, which was generally $40.00.

Meat was the main concern. Mom and Dad insisted we eat as much meat as they could stuff into us. Mom would ask Mr. Gundlock, who was always behind the meat counter, "Carl, would you pick out a couple nice sirloin steaks, four pounds of ground meat, sixteen city chickens, and eighteen cube steaks, and a rolled roast beef?" That last was my favorite. If we had roast beef on Sunday, we'd have roast beef hash on Monday.

Three times a week, Mr. Fitz, the milkman, delivered gallons of milk and dozens of eggs to our back door. The bakery truck stopped twice a week, and each time Mom bought at least two big loaves of spongy white bread for bologna sandwiches, sweet rolls, donuts, and cookies. The cookies were in different shapes. They were soft and moist, but we still dunked them in milk.

★ ★ ★

Fridays were "no meat" days. It was a mortal sin to eat meat from midnight on Thursday until midnight on Friday. A mortal sin meant an eternity in hell. So meat was serious business. Mom always made sirloin steak with onions and mashed potatoes on Thursday nights. She said that way there wouldn't be leftovers to tempt anyone on Friday.

One Friday night shortly after ten o'clock Dad came home agitated. He started to bark at everyone in sight. Joe, Maureen, and I escaped to the kitchen, where Mom was reading the newspaper. I could hear Dad talking on the phone in the other room. He was mad at someone about something, but that wasn't unusual. I heard him say, "You horse's ass. Represent you? Represent you? Are you cracked? You belong in jail. You goddamn drunk. You killed an innocent kid." We heard the slam as Dad hung up the phone.

He charged into the kitchen and without a single word, went to the refrigerator. He took out a big slab of bologna and sliced off two big hunks. Reaching in the bread drawer, he opened the Wonder Bread bag and pulled out two soft pieces. He plunked the bologna on the bread and spread mustard all over it. Only then did Mom look up from the newspaper and notice what he was doing. She jumped up from her chair and said, "Tom, it's Friday. You can't eat that sandwich until after midnight."

"You want to bet? Friday, my ass. Just watch me." He shoved almost a quarter of the sandwich in his mouth. He went back to the refrigerator and took out a cold Heineken, opened it, and took a big slug. He turned to Mom and announced, "I'm going to eat this sandwich, the whole damn thing, and I intend to enjoy every bite of it." With that, he stormed out of the kitchen and headed to the living room with sandwich and beer in hand.

No one said a word. We all knew Dad was going to hell if he died before he could go to confession. Joe, Maureen, and I headed up to our bedrooms, but I didn't sleep. I worried all night that Dad would die and I'd never see him again because he'd be in hell for eternity. Because of a bologna sandwich.

★ ★ ★

I prayed God knew Dad was a good person.

Mom always said, "Actions speak louder than words." And if God was watching Dad, He had to know how much Dad cared about people, especially the underdog.

For all his blowing up, he had the most generous heart of anyone I knew.

Dad would dig into his pockets and give a ten-or twenty-dollar bill to anyone down on his or her luck. If Mom had a cleaning lady who had any problem, and they all did, Dad always showed them respect and tried to help them.

With a houseful of boys, Dad loved it when I brought my

giggling girlfriends home. My friends Bea Hines and Bertie Johannsen (who had a twin brother, Bobby) were cousins and lived only a few blocks from me. They were at 124 often. Dad would dig in his pocket, where he always had loads of change. He would say in a delighted voice, "Girls, now let me see, what is your name? Bertie, oh Bertie, I like those bows in your hair. But let me look at you. Oh my goodness, you look so hungry. Are you hungry, Bertie?"

Shyly, Bertie, blushing and giggling, would say, "Sure, Mr. Murray, if you say so."

"I think you need a chocolate soda, Bertie," Dad would continue. "Now what's your name? Bea, oh, I like that name. But you look like you are hungry too. Let's see, I think you need a banana split." The girls would giggle more. Dad would give each of us a quarter. "Okay girls, Fisher's Drug Store is right down the block and they are waiting for you." And out we would go.

He paid all our college tuitions and bills. My freshman year in college, Dad had seven tuitions to pay, three in undergraduate and four in law school. He was a little grouchy (well, actually, a lot grouchy), but we always knew our tuitions would be paid.

Dad not only fought for the underdog, but also was ready to fight anyone who didn't. I thought God should have liked that.

Our back porch was always available for homeless men—we called them hobos—men who jumped off the train and knocked on our door begging for food.

Dad insisted they be treated kindly. Mom would make a sandwich and find a few cookies. He would say, "Poor soul, there but for the grace of God go I." That was one of both Mom and Dad's common sayings. He would tell these men to sit down on the back porch, and ring the bell if they needed anything else.

I wished I could tell God that my dad was wonderful, even if he said bad words, whipped my brothers (and sometimes my sister), and got mad a lot. It wasn't easy being our dad.

FIRST COMMUNION

On May 3, 1953, my seven-year-old self was certain I was living the biggest day of my life. We began preparing for our First Communion the very first day of the second grade. I was going to be a bride with a veil and a white dress. I would wear long, white stockings that would be held up by a big lady's garter belt.

There were three styles of prayer books to choose from. One had a very small prayer book with no purse, and instead of a real metal cross inside there was only a picture of a cross. It was the least expensive at $1.50. There was a medium-priced style that had a small prayer book and a purse with a scapular and a rosary. It wasn't bad, but the one I dreamed about had six different gifts. The purse held a Mass book with colored pictures of angels, Jesus, Mary, Joseph, and a bishop. There was a white rosary and a tiny little white purse to hold the rosary, a scapular, a chalice pin, and a holy card.

A month before Christmas, all three options were displayed on a table in our classroom. Sister suggested several times a week,

"Boys and girls, this is the perfect gift to request for Christmas." Sister also had veils on sale and highly recommended their purchase. You had to ask permission not to buy the prescribed veil. A few girls asked if they could wear their mother's or older sister's veil. Sister was not happy about this. She begrudgingly granted them permission.

"This will be the happiest day of your life," we were told. "Jesus will take you as His beloved. The angels and saints in heaven along with your parents and friends here on earth will all rejoice for and with you." If that were true, how could anyone buy the cheap prayer book and purse? The biggest day of my life required at least the medium-priced set. But I knew deep down in my heart that I had to get the best one.

Mom told me, "There isn't a bit of difference between the $2.50 and $3.50 package. You'll get the $2.50 one. I'll give you a case for your rosary and a scapular. I have dozens of them." She did. There were drawers full of rosaries, scapulars, prayer books, and holy cards in most every room in our house.

It was true that $3.50 was a lot of money. The average income in 1953 was $1,537.00. A gallon of gas cost twenty-two cents, and a Ford was $1,550.00. But I thought I would die if I couldn't get the one with the real cross. I asked Aunt Sabina, and I asked Dad, and I begged Mom. I showed the pictures of the purses to Aunt Sis at Thanksgiving. She, like Mom, attended Mass daily, and she was the only relative with money. So showing Aunt Sis ensured that the best set would be mine.

Before First Communion we had our first confession, which took months of practice. Sister would say daily, "You will only get the chance once in your life to say these beautiful words: 'Bless me Father for I have sinned, this is my first confession.' So you must say them perfectly."

I was trying to prepare my perfect list of sins, and it wasn't easy. Sister instructed, "Keep your head up and tell your sins, not too loud and not too slow, and, most importantly, not too long." We had to have our list memorized so we wouldn't take too much of Father's time.

Sister asked us if we fought with a brother or sister, told a lie, or said a bad word. I ate an orange Popsicle behind the sofa in the living room and ruined the new carpet. I had cried and covered my face with my hands and said, "I didn't do it."

When Dad accused Joe, he told Dad, "It wasn't me. I didn't eat it, I swear." I started to cry again. Peeking between my fingers. I could see Joe looking at me. To my amazement, I heard him say, "I ate the Popsicle. I did it and I'm sorry. I'll take my punishment." I guessed that was a sin, or maybe even a few, but it was too long to tell. Sister had told us that Father is taking the place of God in the confessional. And I figured since God was all knowing, He probably already knew the details of the Popsicle sin.

Sister also told us a million times, "Say your penance right away. If you say the prayers slowly and sincerely, you can make up to God for your sins. It could shorten your time in purgatory."

There were other ways to shorten our time in purgatory. Helping pagans become Christians was a big plus.

We learned from the first day of school how we could save pagan babies in China. For $5.00, you could buy a pagan baby. That was a lot of money.

But the thought of having my own baby to save from Limbo was overwhelming. Limbo was the place babies went if they were not baptized. Actually, all good people who were not bad enough to go to hell but who were not baptized went to Limbo, too. Limbo was just like heaven, but you didn't get to see God, not even a small peek. And spending eternity looking at God was supposed to be so wonderful that it was worth trying our whole life to be sure we got to heaven.

If I paid the money, the baby was baptized and became a Catholic, no longer a pagan, and was now able to go to heaven with me. The best part was that I was allowed to pick a saint's name for the baby. I would dream every night about my baby, what she looked like, and what I would name her. Sister would send the money and the name I picked to China. A missionary priest who lived there would baptize my baby.

My sister thought she was actually going to get a baby delivered to her at school after she paid her $5.00. She cried and cried when she learned the baby would stay in China. Sister said, "Someday you may be able to visit China and meet your baby, or your baby may come to America. The important issue is you will have all your pagan babies surrounding and thanking you in heaven for eternity."

This was a huge deal every day of school for all eight years. We each had a little pagan baby box with our name on it. Everyone was expected to try to put at least a few cents in their box. You were then allowed to go to the board and add your contribution to your name. Few kids ever got to $5.00, but we all sure tried. I begged Dad and Mom daily for money for the pagan babies. Dad always said, "I have enough of my own babies to feed and clothe. I don't need more babies, especially a Chinese pagan."

★ ★ ★

The night before First Communion always caused tension at 124. You were not allowed to receive communion if you ate or drank anything (including water) after midnight the night before. Before bed, Mom would tie towels around all the sinks in the house to ensure the first communicant didn't forget and take a drink of water. One drop of water after midnight, and the First Communion was called off. So far, Mom had gotten six through the process. She didn't want to take any chances with number seven, her baby girl.

After eight months of daily preparations, we could have accomplished it blindfolded. I could hear Sister's clicker in my sleep. One click, you stand up, two clicks, you sit down, three clicks, and you kneel. We were trained and ready, and I became a bride of Christ.

I had reached the age of reason, which meant I could now commit mortal sin. And that meant I could go to hell for eternity. And heaven was no longer guaranteed. I'd have to earn my way by following all the rules of the church and trying never to sin.

I sometimes wondered if it wouldn't have been easier to die before I reached the age of reason. Then I would go to heaven for sure, and without a life of working for it and maybe not succeeding in the end.

LOVE BY A DIFFERENT NAME

Mom loved us equally, and Dad ignored us equally, at least when we gave him the chance.

I'm not sure why my parents had so many children. It wasn't the kind of question Catholic kids were likely to ask. Birth control pills weren't an option. Even if they had been, Catholics knew it was a mortal sin to use them, and that meant hell for eternity. So I suppose kids beat hell—at least most days.

I had secretly heard that my mom's mother, Christina Cummings, and her only sister, Catherine, our Aunt Sis, frowned every time Dad told them there was another baby on the way.

Seven kids seemed like a lot of work to me, but Mom acted like she loved every minute of it. And being number seven, it was hard not to be grateful they hadn't stopped. Mom always told us, "Every baby God sent was a gift. As each of you were born, I whispered, 'Thank you, God, for sending me this life. Send me as many babies as You want. I will love them with joy, and try my hardest to return each little soul to you. But please, God, never

take a baby from me. I couldn't bear to bury one of my children.'"
Irish Catholic mothers always made contracts with God.

Mom's bargain worked. Babies arrived every year. We were healthy and we all lived through the various germs and broken bones. We rode bikes in the street all over town, drove cars too fast, hitchhiked, and dated crazy people—but we all survived. I never asked Dad what he thought about the nonstop babies. But Mom told us he loved his babies too. Every time he learned another was on the way, he was delighted.

After my arrival, there were no beds for any more children. Joe already slept on a nasty old green sofa in a small bedroom he shared with Jim and Pat.

But I don't think it was Aunt Sis or Grandma Cummings or the bed shortage that ended the babies. I believe Joe and I stopped the baby machine.

★ ★ ★

My sister Maureen was an avid collector. If she saw something she liked, she immediately started to collect more. She collected buffalo nickels and Hallmark doll cards, but one of her favorites was her milk glass animal collection. They were thumbnail-sized, multicolored, and delicate. She told me the milk glass animals would come alive and bite me if I went near them. Maureen never allowed me to touch her things. I had a terrible habit of breaking anything I got near.

The problem was that my bed was right below Maureen's whatnot shelf, which held the little animals. I was afraid to close my eyes. I was sure these creatures would eat me alive. Between the threats of the boogeyman on the porch attached to our bedroom and Maureen's animals, I was terrified of sleeping in my bed.

Mom and Dad had two full-sized beds in their bedroom. Mom

slept in the one closest to the door, and Dad slept in the one next to the window. Every night I would sneak into Mom's bed and sleep with her until morning. Most nights, Joe arrived shortly after me. We both cuddled close to Mom, who slept in a lovely, long silk gown. She smelled like Ivory soap and her skin was like velvet. She was always dead asleep, and didn't seem to even notice we were there. "I am so tired by bedtime," she'd say, "I wouldn't care if the whole city of Sandusky crawled into my bed." During those nights, Joe and I would wet each other and Mom at least once. None of us ever woke up, though. We just slept sweetly, surrounded by Mom's loving arms and pools of warm urine.

One night when I was six years old, I headed for Mom's bed, only to discover the bedroom door was locked. I knocked quietly. Dad opened the door, half asleep, and marched me back to my bed. "Your mommy needs a good night's sleep. You are a second grader now, a big girl. You can't sleep in Mommy's bed anymore." That was the end of my nights with Mom. I was stuck with Maureen, her milk glass animals, and the boogeyman.

★ ★ ★

In 1953, the Korean War ended, Britain crowned a new young queen, Elizabeth II, and the oldest Murray child, Tom, was sixteen, and I, the youngest, turned seven. We were still one of the few families who didn't own a television. The first color TVs had hit the market, but we all knew we'd never get one of those.

One Saturday morning in March, Dad announced, "Come on, everyone, we're going to clean the attic." This was a very untypical activity at 124, so everyone was curious. He dragged some of the boys upstairs and pulled out old suitcases, broken cameras, hats and shoes, busted toys, twisted-up Slinkies, old clothes, and dusty lace curtains that Maureen and I used for playing dress up. We became brides or queens all wrapped up in those curtains.

Dad was shouting orders. "Put this in the Salvation Army pile, suitcases go in that corner. This stuff goes in the trash pile." Then he spied the old blue and white crib with the big rabbit on the headboard. All seven of us had slept in it. After several years in the attic since its last occupant—me—it was dirty and the paint was chipped.

"Okay, boys, that crib and dresser will go downstairs to Mommy's and my bedroom. Here, Pat, grab this side. Joe, get the other side." Tom was at basketball practice, and Bob and Jim, who were always trying to avoid work, had disappeared. Then I heard Joe yelling at the top of his lungs, "Where's Mary? Where's Maureen? I have big news."

I was in the kitchen, sitting on the counter and helping Mom make a coffee cake for the church bake sale on Sunday morning.

Joe finished a thunderous descent down the back steps and shouted breathlessly, "We're going to have a baby. Mary, I mean it. Not a doll, but a real live baby. Where's Maureen? I have to tell her."

Everyone had been drawn to the kitchen by this time. Mom blushed and shyly dropped her eyes. Dad looked like the cat that swallowed the mouse. "Tom," Mom said sweetly, "I thought we agreed to wait as long as possible to tell the children. The baby isn't due for six months. That's forever in a child's life."

"Well, I didn't intend to say anything, but while we were cleaning out the attic I spotted the crib, so it was a perfect time." Dad seemed happier than I'd ever seen him, even happier than when he won money at the racetrack.

Our excitement was overwhelming. We all began asking questions. When will the baby come? Will it be a boy or a girl? Which one do you want? Where will the baby sleep? Can I babysit? Poor Mom couldn't get a moment's peace.

Tom came home from basketball practice in the middle of the excitement. He was reading *Catcher in the Rye* as he walked into the kitchen. He always had a book in one hand and a ball in the other. And he usually seemed preoccupied. Tom wasn't interested in silly kid stuff anymore. He talked about college and Boys State. He knew all about the escalating Cold War, and he discussed Joe McCarthy's hunt for communists in Hollywood with Bob and his friends. Slipping Salinger in his back pocket, Tom asked, "What's all the noise about?"

Maureen, Joe, and I all fought to be the first to tell. Finally, Tom got the message but he didn't join in our excitement. He turned to Mom, and in an accusing tone asked, "Aren't you forty-five years old? Isn't that too old to have a baby? What am I supposed to tell my friends at school? I find this very embarrassing." He grabbed a glass of milk and a couple of cookies and headed upstairs.

Maureen, Joe, and I weren't deterred by his reaction. "Mom, Maureen said she's old enough to babysit, but that I'm still a baby and not old enough to take care of a baby," I said.

"You'd probably break the baby's arms and legs off, just like you did to my bride doll," Maureen accused under her breath.

"I'll need every one of you to help," Mom reassured us.

Joe wanted a boy to play ball with, while Maureen and I dreamed about dressing up our baby sister. But no one was happier than Dad that morning. He was about to turn forty-seven, but he looked like a very young man. And he acted like he was anticipating the arrival of his first baby.

★ ★ ★

When Mom went to church on Sunday, she wore a white maternity top with big black buttons and a black straight skirt. She looked like a cross between the Blessed Mother and a runway model. She never missed daily Mass or a day of caring for Dad and her seven children during her pregnancy.

Six months later, our baby was two weeks past the promised due date. Mom said, as we pestered her daily, "Babies come when God sends them." He chose the evening before the first day of school. I was sound asleep when I heard a commotion in the hall. I saw Mom standing calmly at the top of the steps in her silky gown and robe with her suitcase next to her. Dad was nervous and excited. He decided to pretend to be Jackie Gleason. Poor Mom just stood there while Dad ran up and down the hall swinging his arms from side to side yelling, "And awaaay we go" again and again and again. Finally Mom whispered, "Tom, I think we should go *now*, dear."

Aunt Sabina woke me for school the next morning, and rubbing my head, she said, "Mary you have a baby brother. I know you and Maureen were hoping for a girl, but you'll love your baby brother." She sounded like she was trying to convince herself. And then John Timothy Murray entered our story.

CHRISTMAS TRADITIONS

A cinch belt was on the top of my Christmas list. Maureen was eleven, and she wore a cinch belt, so naturally, I wanted one too.

What I didn't put on my Christmas list was a nurse's kit, even though mine was broken, and all the pieces lost. The only things left were the stethoscope, the uniform that no longer fit, the navy blue cape, and a white cap. I knew better than to even mention the subject, though. My career as a nurse had ended in disaster.

Mabel and Monty Mosey were kids who lived three houses from us on the corner of Columbus Avenue. Mr. Mosey was a photographer, and had his studio in his house. He put all his best pictures in a big showcase window on the front of the house. He changed the pictures every month. Everyone waited to see who would be in his gallery. We loved to see pictures of other Sandusky people looking glamorous, like movie stars. Mrs. Mosey was much younger than her husband, and very protective of Mabel and Monty. They never played with the other kids in the neighborhood. I seldom even saw them.

One day I was really bored and happened to notice Mabel in her yard. I stopped and said, "Hi Mabel, would you like to come to my house and play?" She looked really excited and ran in her house to ask her mom. Mrs. Mosey came out and said, "Mary Catherine, Mabel can come to your house for one hour but she has to take her little brother Monty with her."

That ruined my plans to play dress up with the old lace curtains in our attic. Not knowing what to do with a five-year-old boy, I decided we should play nurse. I put my uniform and cape on, and told Mabel she could be the doctor. We went into our empty garage and set up our examining room in the corner. The garage had oil all over the floor and smelled more like a gas station than a doctor's office. But that didn't bother us.

I started examining Monty. I looked into his eyes, ears, and then his throat. I put a band-aid on a pretend cut on his arm. I took my stethoscope and listened to his heart. Before long I was down to his waist. That's when I decided to go for it and explore the unknown.

I told Monty to pull his pants down. This was the first time I'd ever seen what made a boy a boy. I'd been living with five boys for almost seven years, but we Murrays were very modest. When I saw what was there, I decided I needed to offer a treatment. There was clearly a problem. Monty needed a shot. When he saw me coming at him with the needle, though, he decided he didn't like this game. He pulled up his pants and ran out of the garage, and Mabel followed.

Fifteen minutes later, I heard the phone ring. I heard Mom say, "Well, I will have a talk with Mary. Yes, you're right. You shouldn't let your children play with Mary ever again."

I ran next door to Aunt Sabina's house and stayed as long as I could, but eventually I had to go home and face Mom. She wasn't her usual warm and loving self. All she said was, "Mary, leave the

Mosey children alone. Do you hear me? Do not ever play with them again."

Thus ended my career in the medical profession.

★ ★ ★

That year, Tom was a senior in high school, and I thought he was the most handsome boy I'd ever seen. He was also was my first brother to have a real girlfriend. Tom took his girlfriend, Carol Longer, to Christmas Eve Mass and brought her home after church.

Mom always made Canadian bacon, eggs, and toast for everyone who went to midnight Mass, and Dad was in bed sleeping by then, so things were a lot calmer. Mass didn't end until 1:30 Christmas morning, and the snow was falling as we came out of church. It was so exciting to walk the block and a half home. Every window in our house had a red wreath with a lighted plastic candle in the center. A big Styrofoam Santa hung on the front door. You could see our decorated tree from the street. I couldn't imagine a more beautiful place on earth.

And Santa himself would arrive soon.

But that Christmas Eve I forgot about Santa. I was enchanted with the beautiful Carol Longer. She was petite with short black hair, and she dressed like a movie star. She wore a wool straight skirt and a collarless sweater and pearls. She even smelled good, not like perfume, but like sweet soap. I sat in the booth in our kitchen and just stared at her over my Canadian bacon. She was Audrey Hepburn sitting at my kitchen table. And she was nice, too. She talked to me like I was a real person and not a little kid. That night, instead of dreaming about my Christmas gifts, I dreamt of becoming Carol Longer when I grew up.

★ ★ ★

Christmas morning, Maureen was running around taking loads of pictures with her new Kodak Brownie flash camera. Every time John Timmy moved, there was a flash. Joe got a walkie-talkie that he set up immediately and ordered me upstairs to test it out. Joe and I each got a Slinky every year, which were always twisted beyond repair by the end of Christmas Day. And I got the walking doll I had seen in Specter's and fallen in love with. I could comb her hair and she walked and turned her head. And best of all I got my dream cinch belt. I loved it so much that I refused to take it off regardless of what I was wearing.

Our Aunt Sabina struggled to make ends meet. Her Christmas gifts were practical and useful, but not much fun. She would give Mom a pair of nylon stockings. Maureen and I would get a wool hat or bedroom slippers. She didn't get the boys any gifts.

I loved Aunt Sabina second only to Mom, but Aunt Sis always brought the best gifts. Just like Thanksgiving, each child got a crisp ten-dollar bill, only at Christmas the envelope was tied around a white or milk chocolate Santa. Aunt Sis loved everything expensive and elegant. She brought Maureen and me each a beautiful outfit from Halle's Department Store every Christmas. Since she was a career woman with no husband or children, she could afford them. She brought Mom silky nightgowns and robes that looked more like evening gowns than nightgowns. I'd dress up in them and pretend I was Cinderella.

That Christmas, the world was still infatuated with the newly crowned young Queen Elizabeth II. Everything regal and British was in vogue, and as a result, a popular gift that year was a tea set. Aunt Sis brought me the most wonderful tea set I had ever seen. But the best gift of all was our baby John Timmy, who was now over three months old and lit the entire house with joy. Everyone adored him.

Christmas 1953 I got everything a little girl could dream about:

a walking doll, a real live baby brother, and a cinch belt. I couldn't imagine anything or any place in this world could ever be better than 124 Madison Street was on that day.

I wore my new cinch belt everywhere and with everything. By that point, Mom had given up trying to give me any fashion sense. I wore multiple crinolines under every skirt and dress. Mom tried to get me to tame it down, but like all my siblings, I believed that if a little was good, a lot was better. Moderation wasn't a feature of our gene bank. Thus it was impossible for my seven-year-old self to wear too many crinolines.

I am not sure what God was thinking when he withheld moderation from the Murray line. The problem of excess applied to almost everything. A few weeks before Christmas that year, for example, my father brought a sunlamp home. Several of his eight children were in different stages of puberty, and there were loads of pimples. Dad was always sure he could cure everything better than any doctor, and he intended to cure everyone's pimples with a little sun. There were just two problems. First—there wasn't a ray of sun in Sandusky in December. Worse—the word "little" doesn't exist if you're missing the moderation gene. For the next several weeks, at least one Murray kid arrived at school with some body part sporting a second-degree burn.

Maureen had managed to burn her legs so they looked like a barber pole with red and white stripes. When we returned to school after Christmas, I walked to school beside Maureen looking like a walking lampshade with all my crinolines. They were as painful to sit on as Maureen's sunlamp-burned legs, but I overcame the pain because I knew they made me look so good, especially with my new cinch belt.

THE MAGIC WORD

Dad was certain in his approach to raising children. In his view, there was nothing worse than a spoiled, self-centered child. Children needed to be taught discipline and self-control.

When Dr. Spock emerged as the guru of child rearing in the early 1950s, Dad was livid. "That Dr. Spock is a complete moron. He should be shot. He's going to ruin every child in America. Children are to be seen but not heard." Actually, sometimes I thought Dad would have preferred not to see most of us too often, either.

You were in big trouble if you ever appeared to think highly of yourself. "Who do you think you are, you little piece of importance?" Dad would shout while grabbing you by the collar. If that didn't subdue your delusions of grandeur, Dad would get out his horsewhip and use it.

Dad knew with absolute clarity that he needed to fight the corrupting forces in society that threatened his family. The combined forces of Dr. Spock and television would ruin his children and the American way of life before any nuclear bomb. "TV is destroying the brain of every child in America and turning them into sheep. Baa, baa, baa. That brain-killer will never enter this house. Thinkers, thinkers, thinkers—the world needs thinkers! My children will learn to be thinkers, not sheep," Dad ranted endlessly.

In 1954 there was a lot of talk about the Federal Civil Defense Administration. It was simulating large-scale drills in preparation for a nuclear attack on the United States. They told us the drills were based on the assumption that twelve million Americans would die if it ever happened. That should have captured our attention, but all Maureen, Joe, and I cared about was getting a TV at 124 East Madison.

That was the year I turned eight and was in fourth grade. Along with all my siblings, I felt extremely disadvantaged. We moaned and groaned endlessly, "Everybody has a TV except us." We even annoyed Mom, which was almost impossible. She'd listen to the same woeful story, told over and over by each child. "Everyone was talking about *I Love Lucy*, and I was the only person in the whole school who has never seen it." Lucy, Lucy, Lucy!

★ ★ ★

Summers were often boring at 124, and the most recent one had been no different. Maureen and I had nothing to do. Dad found at least one job for each of his sons, and he imagined his two daughters would help Mom with her chores. I ironed hankies and Dad's boxer shorts. Mom paid me one cent per item. Once a month I glued green stamps into reward books. I usually accumulated at least a dollar a week. But Maureen hated cooking, cleaning, ironing, or anything domestic. She was going into seventh grade, and just beginning to develop. She wanted to spend her summer sunning on the back porch and learning to be cool. Her best friend, Ann, had a job cleaning motel rooms and playing the organ in church for Mass. She was not only busy, but also tired. In any event, she didn't qualify as cool, since she didn't wear a bra and was as naive as Maureen.

Connie Schultz was just the girl Maureen needed to teach her. She was older and developed—mentally and physically. She went to the public school. Connie was thirteen going on thirty, and she used words Maureen had never heard. Her parents both worked, so they had little or no time to monitor Connie's activities. Maureen had spent too much time during the summer hanging out with the cool, fast Connie. Sometimes she even ate dinner at her house. She told me they had something called TV dinners all the time. Maureen said, "They're great, not like the boring food here. And Connie and I sit in front of the TV and eat them. Nobody even cares."

Dad had a sixth sense about people, and he didn't like Connie or her influence on Maureen. With eight children running in and out of our house all day, though, it was easy for Maureen to sneak out and disappear.

★ ★ ★

We knew Mom had finally interceded on our behalf when one day Dad said, "I've decided to buy a TV." We won, finally. *I Love Lucy* was about to arrive at the Murray house. But then reality hit. Dad proudly continued, "I have the perfect solution. The TV will go in Sabina's apartment. You'll be allowed to go to Sabina's on Monday evenings and watch *I Love Lucy*. And you won't lose your ability to think."

The TV was going to be installed next door in our spinster aunt's 800-square-foot apartment. Aunt Sabina adored me and loved to have me sit quietly and visit with her every day and any time. But the boys were different. They were loud and had dirty shoes and made messes. Mom knew Aunt Sabina very well, and while Mom didn't offer her opinion, she did not seem happy about this plan.

The TV was delivered on Saturday, October 2. That Monday, I daydreamed all day about watching my first episode of *I Love Lucy*. It was going to be so exciting. Aunt Sabina had even decided to invite Paul and Mabel Meelfeld, the straight-laced couple that lived in the apartment above her and worked with her at the Heine and Dauch Paper Company.

At 8:55, seven kids trampled one by one across the yard to Aunt Sabina's. She must have spent half her life trying unsuccessfully to get us to take the slightly longer sidewalk route to her building rather than walking across the grass. We arrived with several bangs as the door slammed behind us. There were only two chairs and one sofa in her small living room, so the boys all spread out on the floor.

And at 9:00 p.m. the show began. The TV was a twelve-inch black-and-white RCA, and we thought it was the most amazing thing we'd ever seen. We watched and laughed as Lucy got mixed up in budget problems and sent Ricky into a temper tantrum. Of course, the Mertzs added to the turmoil. That night our world was good. The next day we'd be able to go to school and discuss *I Love Lucy* just like the normal kids.

The first viewing went okay. The next morning, over coffee in our kitchen, Aunt Sabina complained to Mom, "Bob kept annoying everybody, and there were finger marks all over everything in the living room from Joey's sticky fingers. I'm exhausted. It took me an hour to clean up after the kids left last night."

The next Monday came, and once again we descended on Aunt Sabina's tiny living room with sticky fingers, annoying Bob, and the Meelfelds for another installment of *I Love Lucy*. About ten minutes into the show—just at the moment Lucy was pretending to be Bessie the maid to impress one of Ricky's guests—the TV lost its picture. Joe jumped up to try to fix it. He wiggled and jiggled the antenna, but all we saw was snow. Then, with her cherub face and sweet, innocent voice, Maureen stood up and shouted, "Oh fuck."

There was complete silence. Even the boys were speechless.

A few days later, a delivery truck from Brownsworth's Appliances pulled up in front of 124 East Madison and out came a new nineteen-inch TV. The deliveryman set it up in the corner of our living room, and there it stayed for the rest of our days.

I worried a lot about mortal sins, not just for myself, but also for my whole family. I had to. Dying with a mortal sin on your soul condemned you to hell for eternity. I couldn't imagine basking in heaven, enjoying eternal happiness, while looking down on one or all of my siblings burning in hell.

I thought I knew quite a bit about mortal sins. You went straight to hell if you ate meat on Friday, went inside a Protestant church, missed Sunday Mass, had sex, or murdered someone. I never ate meat on Friday. I averted my eyes whenever I walked by a Protestant church. I went to Mass every Sunday and every other day of the week, except Saturday. At the advanced age of eight, I'd never had sex or killed anyone, and couldn't imagine I ever would.

But this day, I discovered a brand new sin. I learned that attending a public school was also a mortal sin.

Shortly before school was about to start that year, I was attending Sunday Mass. Since every word was in Latin, I always found it a struggle to sit and kneel quietly and pay attention for an hour. The sweetest lady in the church, Mrs. Rossi, always sat next to me at Sunday Mass. She would smile at me, and I thought she really liked me, but I wasn't 100 percent sure. She didn't have a tongue, so she never said anything. She held a big white men's hankie up to her mouth to stop her from drooling.

Bored to death by Mass and Mrs. Rossi, I picked up the bulletin and began to read.

```
* * *
SERVERS' SCHEDULE                 AUGUST 9 - 14
   6:30  -  JOSEPH ESPOSITO & ROBERT SIDNER
   7:00  -  LAWRENCE STOOKEY & DAVID QUILTER
   7:30  -  JOE  Da GIAU & RICHARD MARCHUS
HOLY COMMUNION AT 7:30 MASS: JOSEPH GENNARI
                   * * *
     SCHOOL REOPENS IN JUST ONE MONTH. We expect
EVERY CHILD OF THE PARISH TO BE ENROLLED IN THE
CATHOLIC SCHOOL THIS YEAR. It is DIOCESAN LAW
for all Catholic children to be enrolled in the
Catholic School when one is available.
     Our Parish school is adequate to care for
every child in the Parish. It is as well equipped
and well staffed as any school in the City.
     PLEASE NOTE WELL that no permission ever
given by anyone in the past is valid for this
year. Permission of the Pastor must be had for
children to attend the public school. THIS OB-
LIGATION IS A SERIOUS ONE, BINDING UNDER PEN-
ALTY OF EXCLUSION FROM THE SACRAMENTS.
```

My heart stopped when I read the last paragraph. My family was going to hell! My brother Jim would begin Sandusky High in September. Tom and Bob had been attending the public high school for the past couple of years.

I panicked and started to pray really hard. But I wasn't sure who exactly was going to hell. Would my parents go to hell for sending my brothers to a public school? Would my brothers go to hell for going? Or would they all be damned to eternal fire?

I ran home after church, and all out of breath, showed Mom the bulletin. Crying I said, "Are the boys going to hell? Are you and Dad going too?" Mom was busy frying Canadian bacon and eggs in anticipation of the next five kids arriving home from Mass and looking for breakfast. But when she saw how upset I was, she stopped and looked at the bulletin.

Not the slightest bit concerned, she said, "Dear, don't worry. Dad got Monsignor Foran's permission for the boys to attend Sandusky High. Our family is not allowed to attend Saint Mary's. It is a German National School and we're Irish. Only people with German blood are allowed there."

I had heard Dad talk endlessly about the Irish being discriminated against, but now I learned that even some Catholics didn't like us because we were Irish and not German.

DAD LOST

One afternoon when I was perhaps ten or eleven years old, I was heading down the back steps toward the kitchen, the nerve center of 124 East Madison. I heard Dad coming in the back door. You always heard Dad before you saw him, but this day he was uncharacteristically quiet. I decided to become invisible. The back steps leading down to our kitchen were a great place to hear secrets.

I just had a small glimpse, but I saw Dad pulling his linen hankie out of his pocket and wiping tears from his eyes. Then he straightened his back as he walked into the kitchen looking for Mom.

Mom was sitting in the living room reading the morning paper and enjoying a rare break from kids and kitchen. She had already peeled the potatoes, cleaned the beans, and made junket for dessert. Mom made dessert every night—warm apple pie with big scoops of Otto's vanilla ice cream on top, brownies, chocolate chip or peanut butter cookies, or our favorite, Duncan Hines devil's food cake with homemade chocolate frosting.

Mom looked up and smiled. "Hi, dear, you're home early."

Dad straightened his back again and bravely said, "No cause of action." This was a legal term, but we all knew it meant Dad lost his case.

"Tom, I'm so sorry. You worked like a dog on that case. What happened?"

"I don't know," Dad said. "The facts were a little blurry, but mostly on our side. If I could have gotten just one Negro on that jury, it would have changed everything. I feel like I let Orville down. Poor guy, never once in his whole life has he gotten a break. I thought I was going to change that for him."

"You did your best, Tom. You couldn't have done anything more. Will Orville and his family be okay?"

"Oh sure, he's a survivor. He and that little wife will figure out how to go on," Dad continued, choking back tears, "but I just hoped I could get him what he deserved. God only knows he deserved compensation for his injuries."

"Tom, you spent over a month working day and night on this. I know you are disappointed, but you just have to accept it. Sit down and relax, and try to put it out of your mind."

"Don't worry, Peggy. We'll still eat. I have all the apartments rented. The rents will cover the bills this month."

"I know we'll be fine. God has never let us down."

Dad had begun purchasing apartment buildings in 1940, shortly after he bought 124 East Madison and his fourth child, Pat, was born. Dad knew the legal business could have long dry spells. With lots of mouths to feed and brains to educate, he wanted a steady source of income. By the time I was born in 1946, Dad had several small apartment buildings.

"Well, I should have said all the rents except that poor soul, Rita, in the Adams Street apartment. She was coming into the courthouse today as I was leaving. When she saw me, she started to cry. She was holding an ice pack up to her mouth. Her tooth was aching. That bum she married has left again. I told her to stop by the office tomorrow and I'd see what I could do. I'll ask John Schaffer to fix her tooth. I hate to ask, he has all those mouths to feed himself. But he's really such a good guy, I know he'll do it gladly." Dr. Schaffer had his dental office across from Dad's office in the Murray and Murray Law building. They bartered services. Our ten mouths got dental care, and Dr. Schaffer got free rent and any legal work he needed.

"I'll call Sister Lucia at Providence Hospital and see if she can find Rita a job," Dad continued. "In the meantime, I told her not to worry about the rent. I know she'll pay me if and when she can."

"Of course, Tom, you're right. The poor thing."

With that, Dad announced, "I'm going back to work, Peggy. Save a piece of steak for me, and put a beer on ice. I'll be home no later than seven. Now give me a hug."

But before Dad left he stopped in the kitchen, and taking a pair of scissors out of the drawer, he headed to the backyard. A few minutes later, Dad reappeared with a beautiful, long-stemmed red rose he had cut from his prized rosebush.

Handing it to Mom he said, "The most beautiful rose from my garden for the most beautiful woman in the world. You are not only beautiful, but you are the best wife a man could ever have."

With that, Dad flew out the front door, a new person, ready to once again take on the world. T. J. Murray was down, but never out.

MAUREEN ENTERS POLITICS

Dad exercised and dieted every day. He had a record player in his bedroom, and he did sit-ups with "The Bridge over the River Kwai" blasting every morning. Dad would try to stay at 170 pounds, but Dad loved food, and an unwanted ten pounds regularly plagued him.

He'd call Mom to describe every bite of food he ate at lunch, always ending with, "So Peggy, nothing for dinner tonight." Mom would hang up the phone, go to the kitchen, and defrost something nice for Dad's dinner that evening. And he always arrived home starving. He continued losing and gaining those ten pounds for his whole life.

What energy Dad didn't expend exercising he burned in passion. "That horse's ass Eisenhower! Stevenson has more brains in his little finger than Eisenhower has in that big empty bald head of his." Dad had run for the United States Congress in 1942 and had been defeated. However, he never lost his high-spirited love of politics, defending the underdog, or maybe just a good fight.

I wouldn't have paid any attention to his political talk if it hadn't been for Maureen. It was a few weeks before the 1956 presidential election and we were all sitting in the kitchen eating dinner. Dad was raging, "Those damn Republicans are using the war and communism to scare the American people into voting for a military man."

Most of us were just eating our mashed potatoes and city chicken smothered in gravy without paying attention to his commentary. But Maureen, trying to join in, said, "Sister Felicia said no Catholic is allowed to vote for Adlai Stevenson because he's divorced. And divorce is a mortal sin."

That ended dinner. Dad jumped up from the table and threw his napkin on his plate. With his face turning blood red and spewing out every bad word in his repertoire, he darted into the dining room and picked up the phone. He shouted so loud that if the windows had been open, the nuns who lived two blocks away could have heard him without mechanical intervention. "Operator, give me Saint Peter and Paul's Convent. Yes, goddammit, Jackson Street."

Maureen became hysterical. She was crying and begging, "Please, please stop him, Mom. Sister will kill me tomorrow. She'll punish me or flunk me."

Fortunately for Maureen—and perhaps for all the rest of us who had to spend our days with the Sisters—no one answered the phone at the convent.

A MIRACLE, PLEASE

We had a saint for everything. Saint Jude helped when we thought our cause was hopeless. Saint Anthony found our lost stuff. I relied on him all the time. I'd repeat, "Tony, Tony, look around. Something's lost and must be found." And just like that the lost object would appear. Not always, but sometimes.

By this time, a group of us girls had been palling around for several years. Patricia Reilly, Molly Brown, Jane Kowalski, Bea Hines, Bertie Johannsen, and I went almost everywhere together. I must have slept at each of their houses at least a dozen times. Molly's cousin Louise Brown came along, too. She went to Saint Mary's, but lived next door to Molly. She was always at Molly's slumber parties, and we all felt like she was part of our gang. None of us had begun to develop in any noticeable ways.

I was in sixth grade, and I wanted breasts. As hard as I thought about it, I couldn't come up with a saint who could help. Then I remembered Saint Agnes. Maureen chose Agnes as her confirmation name because she said, "Saint Agnes is so powerful. She can do anything. When she was a young girl, a bunch of men were trying to destroy her chastity. They made her stand naked. She prayed and her hair grew instantly and covered her entire body. And all the men who were staring at her were struck blind."

If Saint Agnes could accomplish all that, surely the breasts I wanted—just average, not gigantic—would be a snap.

By then, a few girls in my class (mostly the Italians) were starting to wear a bra. We all wanted not just the bra, but also something to fill it. Even the slightest sign of growth was hopeful. We all knew our popularity with the boys would soar, and the bigger the better.

The Italians seemed more informed and comfortable about sex than the rest of us. Anthony Caldrone would run his hand over our backs and announce to everyone in hearing distance which girl was wearing a bra. "Bea is wearing a braaaw," he'd shout. "Bertie has a new braaaw today." Or, "Molly isn't wearing a braaaw." We'd all run if we saw him coming, but Anthony was clever and knew how to sneak up on you. Molly was so fearful of his assaults that she wore a sweater over her blouse every day so Anthony's bra test would fail if he tried it on her.

At the beginning of the school year, Diana Drake, a petite and delicate blond girl, raised her hand and said, "Sister, may I please be excused?" Diana was really smart and never wanted to miss a minute of class. But on that day, she left the classroom flat chested and returned a few minutes later proudly sporting ample breasts.

It didn't take long before everyone noticed. First Leno Conti started to point and giggle. Before long everyone was snickering and pointing.

Diana's much-too-large toilet paper breasts didn't last long. Within two minutes, they'd started a slide down to her waist. Poor Diana began to cry. Sister Yvonne finally intervened, "Diana, please wait outside in the hall."

Sister then turned to our class and with a stern voice and cold stare said, "Stop this minute. Carmen Calderone, come up here and monitor the classroom. If I hear as much as one sound, you will all be in this classroom during recess for the rest of this year. Open your religion book to the Ten Commandments, and begin to copy each one in silence." With that, she stormed out of the room.

Several minutes later Diana returned, flat chested. She sat down at her desk, humiliated.

★ ★ ★

Once a month, my best friends Molly Brown and Patricia "Pat" Reilly would each bring a note that said, "My daughter has my permission to go to Mary Murray's house for lunch today."

When the lunch bell rang at 11:30, the three of us would head out of school in the direction of 124, but instead of turning right on Columbus Avenue, we'd turn left and walk downtown to the Woolworth's lunch counter. We'd order an egg salad, grilled cheese, or bacon and tomato sandwich. Molly loved the hot dogs that came in toasted bread that was shaped like a bun. They all came with French fries, and we'd each order a chocolate milk shake. We ate, giggled, and talked about boys.

On one occasion, Patricia and I had gone to the Ohio Theatre the Saturday before our lunch to see a movie. We hadn't told our parents that we were meeting Gusty and Johnny, the coolest boys in our class, at the movies. We sat in the back row—Patricia with Johnny, and me with Gusty. That day I experienced my first kiss.

Molly was a great audience at our Woolworth's lunch. She was anxious to hear every detail about our adventure. We promised that the next time, she could come too.

Molly was petite and Patricia was thin. Neither of them loved food like I did. They never ate more than half their lunches. I decided to save some of my lunch money each time we went to Woolworth's. I'd just eat whatever food Molly and Patricia left.

I planned to secretly buy a bra at Woolworth's after one of our lunches. After a couple of months of my lunch-sharing plan, I had the $2.50, but not the nerve to go to the counter and pick out a bra. That counter in the dime store was almost as forbidden as the *Playboy* and *Esquire* section in Gray's Drug Store. I was deathly scared that someone would see me and tell my mom or my sister. But bolstered by Patricia and Molly, I finally decided to take the big step.

"Just walk up to the counter and if anyone says anything, tell the clerk your ma told you to buy this," Pat suggested. We never said the B word. The very thought of saying "bra" or "brassiere" to an adult terrified me. Even when I was much older and allowed to watch late-night TV shows with my brothers, I lived in mortal fear of a bra commercial coming on. It would have been so embarrassing to see a woman wearing a bra in the presence of a boy, even a brother. It was such a worry that I'd leave the room during every commercial.

"What if they ask my name or my phone number and then call my mom?" I asked.

"Just say your name is Diana Drake and give her a fake phone number. We can run out of the store while the clerk tries to call." Patricia was so smart. She had the best ideas.

After lunch, the three of us pretended to be looking at bobby pins, hairnets, and bows. Then we slid over to the jewelry counter and pretended to be very interested in the ID bracelets. We chatted about having our names engraved on one. We avoided the candy counter. The woman who worked there wore a white uniform and weighed about 200 pounds. She had no teeth and never smiled. She guarded the orange slices, spearmint leaves, and chocolate kisses like the Gestapo. She screamed if any kid got close to touching the plastic shields over the candy. If you wanted candy, you had to stand with your hands at your side and ask her. She would take her shovel, and without any expression on her face, dig into the tray as if she was digging for gold. She would then weigh the candy and put it in a small white bag. You had to pay her before she handed you the candy.

As we got closer and closer to the bra counter, I got more and more nervous. Finally I walked over and picked one up. I didn't even look at the size. I just grabbed one that looked like it would fit. I'd make it work.

I handed it to the skinny sales clerk. She looked like a skeleton and smelled like a tobacco factory. She never even looked at me. She just took my money and put the bra in a brown paper bag and handed it to me as she continued chomping on her gum. We darted out of the dime store like three shoplifters. I headed back to school with my prize, the ultimate sixth-grade status symbol, stuffed in my coat pocket.

I wore that bra every day. When I got home, I would run upstairs and take it off. I hid it in the back of a drawer that was filled with my brothers' old underwear.

Two years after my anxiety-filled shopping trip to Woolworth's, I opened the top drawer of my dresser. There were two training bras from Spector's sitting next to my underpants, T-shirts, and slips. I never asked, and Mom never said a word. I just assumed they were for me.

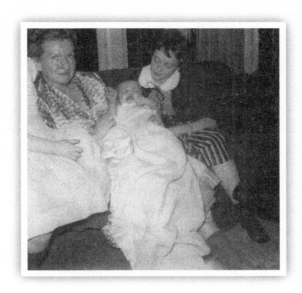

HEARTBREAK HOTEL

Dad was a different kind of Catholic than Mom. He went to church on Sunday, to the last Mass at 11:00, while Mom went every morning. I didn't like to attend Mass with Dad. He'd get out of his pew during Mass and tell any kid who was goofing off in church—not just his own—to be quiet or get out. The potential for embarrassment didn't stop there. Dad had hemorrhoid surgery several times. Most people would have skipped Mass until they recovered, but not my dad. He walked into church carrying his big orange inner tube, and placed it on the seat in his usual pew.

Other than his attendance at Sunday Mass, I don't remember Dad doing much else Catholic. He sent the nuns a big slab of Canadian bacon at Christmas, and he supported the church and the school with money.

He thought men who were members of the Knights of Columbus, a Catholic fraternal organization, were nuts—almost as bad as the Masons. Unlike Mom, he didn't hesitate to criticize a nun or a priest if they did something he thought was stupid or mean spirited.

He screamed the loudest I had ever heard when the convent in Villa Marie Pennsylvania called and said, "Mr. Murray, your sister, Sister Francelia died last night." Dad banged the phone down and shouted, "SON OF A BITCH. Those goddamn nuns never even told me Gert was sick. I am going to kick their asses when I get to that convent." This went on until we all got to the convent. Dad didn't kick anyone, but he wasn't exactly sweet either.

It was hard to tell much about Dad's faith. It seemed to me that most of what he did was because he loved Mom. However, once in a while he'd catch our attention.

Good Friday was the only day Mom made a big issue out of our behavior. We were expected to go to church for the Stations of the Cross or quiet prayers. We couldn't even think about playing with a friend or going to a movie, even if it was a holy one, like *The Robe* or *The Song of Bernadette*. Between noon and 3:00 p.m. we were supposed to be quiet and prayerful. After three, things loosened up a bit, but going on a date or to a friend's house was still off-limits that day.

Since we had the day off from school, we were all anxious to have some fun—more fun than attending the Stations of the Cross or praying for three hours. The older boys generally managed to make themselves scarce, but Maureen, Joe, and I were usually just bored.

On Good Friday in 1956, Elvis Presley was the newest, hottest deal in our world. In January he had released his first gold-record song, "Heartbreak Hotel." Maureen's friend Bev had just gotten a 45 recording of it and she lent it to Maureen for the day. Around noon, Maureen decided to get her little record player out and listen to Bev's record. Joe and I were just wandering around. I wanted to decorate Easter eggs and Joe wanted to be outside on his bike. Since we couldn't do either until after three, we decided to lurk outside Maureen's bedroom, so we could listen, too.

She played it over and over again because she had to return it to Bev, whom she would meet at church at 2:30. We all wanted to listen every possible minute until then. After listening for half an hour, Joe and I knew all the words by heart, and we were getting sick of hearing, *You make me so lonely, baby, I get so lonely, I get so lonely, I could die.*

Suddenly, we heard Dad coming up the stairs in a rage. He banged open the door and with his face blood red shouted, "Girlie, where did you get that filthy music? This is Good Friday, and you think listening to that dirty, filthy Presley is okay?" He took the record off the player and smashed it into bits. Maureen became hysterical. That ended our prayerful Good Friday.

CEDAR POINT, BERARDI'S, AND THE BACK PORCH

Summer was almost here, and I couldn't wait. By now I hated school and just wanted it to end. I had struggled for five years to hide my reading issue, but now school just bored me to death.

As always, Patricia (my longtime pal) and I had planned every detail of our annual last day of school. Patricia would sleep over at my house. Sleep was not exactly what we did. Neither of us could sleep with all the excitement. We mostly ate brownies and talked nonstop about what we would do the next day at Cedar Point.

Going to Cedar Point was like going to heaven. It was the best amusement park in the world, at least our world. It only had about six rides—the merry-go-round, the octopus, the bug, the tilt-a-whirl, and the bullet—but those were enough to thrill us for a whole day. Cedar Point also had Berardi's French fries (the best in the world) and things we never got anywhere else: cotton candy and candy apples. Finally polio was now mostly under control at least in the United States, so we could go to Cedar Point any time we wanted. When the school year ended, I could look forward to three whole months of doing nothing but swimming, baking cookies and brownies, going to Cedar Point, and sitting on Aunt Sabina's back porch. Life would be perfect.

★ ★ ★

By the time May arrived, we always had a few amazingly warm days. We all dreamed about those first warm days of spring during the long, gray winter months.

These were the days we'd get our bikes out and take our first ride for the season. We would dig into our dresser drawers and find our summer clothes, regardless of how cool it was or where they were buried.

The previous fall, Mom had put the shorts Maureen had outgrown in my drawer. I was always thrilled to get any of Maureen's clothes. I dreamed that I would look like her in them. I didn't, but I never gave up hope.

I had those thunder thighs and a big butt. And no matter what I did, they both seemed to get bigger every year.

I found my favorite pair of Maureen's old Bermuda shorts. I had loved those on Maureen. They were navy blue with red pin stripes. They were really the kind you would wear to Cedar Point or a slumber party, not around the house. But I was afraid it could be a few weeks before we would get another warm day, so I was going to wear these great shorts at least once.

I ran down the back stairs to the kitchen yelling, "Hey Mom, look at me. It's summer." Mom said, "Well, you may be rushing it a bit, but they look cute on you." She looked at me kind of sadly and said, "Oh those pants fit you perfectly. Maureen wore those just last summer. Don't grow up too fast. You know you are my baby girl." I knew only too well that before long, I would be bigger than Maureen. People already said, "Look at Mary. She is going to be a much bigger girl than Maureen." It was not a happy thought.

Mom, handing me a pan and a bag of beans, said, "Now, fancy pants, how about sitting here at the table and cutting the ends off the green beans."

I plunked down on the chair. As my eyes dropped to admire my new shorts, horror struck my heart. I was paralyzed. I just stared at my exposed thighs. What happened to them? And when did it happen?

I screamed, "Mom, Mom look at my legs. What are those?" Of course I knew what they were. Mom had varicose veins all over her legs. But she had eight children and she was old. I was only ten.

Fighting back tears, I said, "Mom, what am I going to do?"

Mom calmly said, "Oh, those are just a few small veins. They are nothing to worry about. No one will ever notice them."

I dashed up to Mom's bathroom and tried to cover them up with Mom's dried-up pancake makeup, which she never used. That didn't work. I got makeup all over the tops of my now favorite shorts, which called even more attention to my thighs. God seemed to have no mercy when it came to my body.

The veins were right at the spot where my Bermuda shorts ended. My skin was snow white, and when I sat down, all I could see were purple lines. Of course there would be no hiding them when I was in a swimsuit.

I now had another secret to hide. I bought a big straw purse for summer. It went everywhere with me. It sat on my lap covering my plump, vein-streaked thighs. And inside that purse I carried a copy of Maureen's *Seventeen* magazine that I could pull out and plunk on my lap as a shield of last resort.

SISTER OF MY DREAMS

Because enrollment was down, Saint Mary's Parish had finally decided to allow the inferior parishes to send their mostly Italian, Polish, and Irish students to their far superior German school.

My sister was the first one in our family to attend high school at St. Mary's. In order to be democratic, they decided the freshman class should have one cheerleader from each school. My sister got to be the one from Saint Peter and Paul's.

But in 1956, her sophomore year, one of those three girls would be chosen to be THE cheerleader who never had to try out again. She would be guaranteed her spot until her senior year. At that time she would become the head honcho cheerleader. Maureen wanted that lauded spot.

Maureen went into her secluded mode, deciding not to socialize, and just lay low at 124. She would sun on the back porch, which was attached to her bedroom, and read books. She wasn't old enough to get a real job, so she almost immediately got bored.

And that was where I came in. Maureen decided she knew how

she would get cheerleading. She would ask God for a miracle.

We had heard and read about endless miracles, so this made perfect sense. But she needed to figure out the perfect path to getting this specific miracle.

Maureen was a night owl. She stayed up late reading (and whatever else she did). Getting up in the morning was torture for her.

Out of the blue, Maureen sweetly said, "Hey Mare, come upstairs and play Parcheesi with me." No more needed to be said. Like lightning, I was there with the game in my hands.

Maureen said, "I'll set the game up. You go downstairs and get us some Pepsi and pretzels."

I was so happy. I ran down the back stairs. I couldn't wait.

While we were playing, Maureen said, "How about doing something with me this summer?" It didn't matter what she would have asked, I would have done it.

Maureen told me this long, sad story about how she really wanted to get cheerleading, but knew she didn't have a chance. Cheerleading was the most important position a girl could achieve in high school. *Seventeen* magazine had two cheerleaders on its cover in July 1956. Every girl wanted to be a cheerleader.

Maureen said, "I have to compete against Betsy Boehner, the best looking and most popular girl in my class, and Colleen Moyer, the second best looking and popular girl in my class. The boys on the football and basketball teams will vote. I don't have a chance against those girls. The boys call me a cold fish, and they adore those two. It would require a miracle for me to win."

I adored her. She was the most beautiful girl I knew. And when she wasn't being mean to me, or acting like a witch, we had lots of fun together. But now she was being nicer to me than ever before. I immediately began to feel sorry for Maureen, and I wanted to help her win.

Maureen said, "I will make a deal with you. If you wake me up every morning for 8:00 Mass, and if you go with me, and pray for me to get cheerleading, I will let you sleep in my room all summer. And I will play Parcheesi or Clue with you every night."

This was a no-brainer for me. I said, "Yes, yes, yes."

So I moved into Maureen's room for the summer. Every morning, I woke her up and we walked together to church. On the way she would say, "Don't forget, when Father puts the host on your tongue, say, 'Please God, give my sister Maureen cheerleading.' Promise?" Over and over I promised, mortal sin on my soul. Then she would say, "Tell me what you are going to say."

Over and over I would say, "I will beg Jesus to give you cheerleading." And I did, mortal sin on my soul.

Maureen and I played either Parcheesi or Clue every night. She would send me downstairs to get Pepsi and pretzels. She would look at the clues or move her Parcheesi token while I was gone. Or she would refill my glass of Pepsi so often, I would have to go to the bathroom nonstop. In any event, Maureen figured out how to win every game. I didn't have a competitive bone in my body. I loved playing with my sister, and I couldn't have cared less who won.

The summer ended, and I had loved almost every moment.

We headed back to school. I was starting the seventh grade.

The previous senior class at Maureen's school had several girls, including a few cheerleaders, who ended their senior year pregnant. There was shotgun wedding after shotgun wedding that summer.

Father Etzel decided to make a change in cheerleading rules. HE would choose the girl who would get the forever-cheerleading spot, not the boys. And he picked my sister, the cold fish. Maureen got her miracle!

SEX AT 124

I walked in the door of 124 East Madison and smelled death.

The aroma of ham laced with pineapple rings and maraschino cherries baking in the oven could mean only one thing. Someone had died.

Dad had been born and raised in Sandusky, and when anyone he knew had a death in their home—and Dad knew everyone—Mom baked a ham to send to the family. The hams were beautiful, and the smell made you want to grab a knife and dig in. But I never actually got to taste one of Mom's bereavement hams. Dad would pull his car into the driveway (he never turned the car motor off), run into the house, and like lightning, whisk this picture-perfect ham out the front door. All that remained was that fabulous sweet and salty smell.

I headed right to the kitchen and didn't even take my coat off. Mom was there in her starched housedress and her multicolored cobbler apron.

"Hi, Mom. Who died?"

She laughed. "No one died. Mary Sernek is coming home from the hospital today, and her husband George is just lost. He has never done a thing in the kitchen. Mary had such a nasty surgery, and the poor thing has a long and painful recovery ahead of her. She is such a peach." That was the term Mom used for only a few special women she liked a lot.

I asked what I thought was a logical question. "What's wrong with her?"

Dead silence filled the kitchen. My mother, her face turning bright red, looked away and whispered in an embarrassed voice, "Oh, female problems."

"Female problems" meant the unspeakable subject: sex. I knew not to ask any more questions. Some part below Mrs. Sernek's neck and above her legs had a problem, one of the unmentionable parts.

Medical problems were, for the most part, discussed openly in our house. Dad had surgery for hemorrhoids. Aunt Sabina had heart surgery. Uncle Louie (not a real uncle, but a friend of our family and a hopeless alcoholic) suffered from cirrhosis of the liver. Even Aunt Lucille's frontal lobotomy wasn't a secret. And the discussion about how Uncle Louie got cirrhosis of the liver or why Aunt Lucille had a frontal lobotomy (while seldom discussed) were not taboo, like sex.

The aura of silence surrounding sex was powerful and always present, both at home and at school. Consequently, our small minds were endlessly occupied trying to find out something about "IT."

★ ★ ★

No one explained anything about anything. Breasts appeared, hair started to grow under your arms and in other strange places, and you began to bleed. You were just supposed to be surprised and figure it out for yourself.

One day, I was in our kids' bathroom and happened to spot the blue Q-tip box in the wastebasket. It looked stuffed with something. Before I got it halfway open, I freaked out. There were two thick, gauzy pads soaked in blood.

By then, Maureen, now a teenager, hated me more than ever. I was once again kicked out of what was supposed to be our bedroom. Maureen tried hard to never see me or talk to me. She stayed in our bedroom next to the bathroom alone most days. I found her, squirreled away on her bed, reading a movie star magazine about the life of Ann Blyth, her favorite movie star. Her two main concerns then were movie stars and dreaming about being married to Mr. Spector, the tall, dark, and handsome man who owned the all-purpose store downtown. As expected, she was annoyed by my interruption, but I couldn't ignore a wastebasket full of blood.

"Maureen, get up and come into the bathroom, please, fast," I said, panicked. Maureen reluctantly put her magazine down and got up and poked her head into the bathroom.

"You idiot. What the heck is your problem?"

Afraid to touch the mess, I said, "Look, there's blood in the wastebasket." Maureen looked guilty, as if she might have killed one of my brothers. I knew there were at least three she would have taken out gladly. She recovered quickly and said, "Promise you won't tell Mom or Dad?" I promised. "No, not just a promise, say mortal sin on my soul."

"Mortal sin on my soul," I swore.

"Pat was playing with the knife, the one in Dad's top drawer." That was the secret knife we were never supposed to know was there. "Jim grabbed it and tried to pull it away and accidentally stabbed Pat in his side. He bled like crazy but he's okay now. Don't mention it to anyone, or they'll both be in big trouble."

At dinner that evening, Pat looked so normal, and so did Jim. I kept trying to get a peek of Pat's side or discover any sign of blood. There was no sign of anything, not even a Band-Aid. Neither brother looked concerned or guilty.

★ ★ ★

It was at least another year before my friend Bertie snuck the book *You Are Becoming a Woman* out of her house and brought it to our slumber party. "Don't tell anybody I showed you this book," she said when she pulled it out of her overnight bag. "I'd be in big trouble."

"We're going to do *what* for five days every month for the rest of our lives?" I asked Bertie as she read the pertinent chapter. It had to be a bad joke or something. Like a light switch, it dawned on me what that blood in the bathroom was, and where it had come from.

Bertie started to giggle. "Look, it says so right here. It's called menstruation or your period, and after it starts, you can have a baby." I liked that part. My little brother John was no longer a baby. I thought it would be fun to have my own baby.

Suddenly we heard noise in the hall outside the bedroom. "Be quiet, be quiet, hide the book," I said, panicked at the thought of anyone finding out what we were reading—especially my tattle-tale sister.

THE BROWN BAG

I was twelve, and the Explorer I satellite was about to be launched. It was now 1958, and the nuns were using the occasion to try to get us all excited about science and math. But we were more interested in Elvis Presley, who was being drafted and would be serving in Germany. We were devastated. How could we live without Elvis?

Christmas was over, and we had just returned to school after our two-week holiday break and all the girls were proudly wearing the new clothes they'd received for Christmas. We were now old enough to care about only two things: boys and clothes. I was wearing my yellow wool straight skirt and matching sweater. I'd begun to develop, and I hated my thighs and my butt. They had both become plump and I wanted to be skinny, like my friend Bea, and have big breasts, like Veronica. Instead, my butt and thighs were the only parts growing, and at a rapid pace.

Lunch break ended, and we all stood to say our afternoon prayer and sing the national anthem before we started our math lesson. Suddenly, I felt a warm gush between my legs. It felt like

I was wetting my pants. I was afraid to ask to be excused so soon after lunch, but I was more afraid of what my pale yellow skirt would look like.

The Murrays had an unfortunate history with my teacher, Sister Virgilia. My brother Joe had had several fights with her. The day he graduated from the eighth grade, he knocked on Sister Virgilia's classroom door and announced, "Before I leave this school, I want to say one thing to you sister: Go to hell." Then he thumbed his nose, and shouted "Nana nana na na" as he ran out of the building. He shared similar farewells with almost all the nuns. And Maureen had been accused of calling Sister Virgilia "stretch nose" and "pop-eyed"—and all the nuns "booze dozers."

I'd had my own run-in with Sister Virgilia a year earlier. Some of the girls were helping our teacher, Sister Yvonne, set up the supplies for our Friday afternoon art class. I had made fudge the night before, and brought it to school to share with the girls. As I opened the wax paper it was wrapped in, all the girls dove at it. There was only one big piece left when Patricia came into the classroom carrying an empty water glass. She screamed and ran toward the fudge. (Patricia was mad about fudge and brownies.)

I never wanted to miss a chance to have some fun. I grabbed the fudge and ran out of the room. Patricia was on my heels like a pit bull. She was shouting as she chased me down the hall, "Give me that fudge." I headed up the steps and ran into the girls' bathroom. Bea, Bertie, and Jane had followed just to watch the show.

We were all laughing and squealing. Running into a stall, I locked the door. Patricia, who had been my best friend since the first grade, went into the stall next to me and stood on the toilet. She still had a glass in her hand. Patricia was looking down on me as I sat on the toilet pretending to eat the last hunk of fudge. "If you eat that fudge, Mary, I'll pour toilet water on your head," Patricia shouted, causing an eruption of laughter from our growing audience and me.

Suddenly, there was total silence. I mean frighteningly dead silence.

Then I heard the voice from hell. "Get down from that toilet and come out this minute, Miss Reilly. What do you think you are doing in there, girlie?" Sister Virgilia demanded. I heard Patricia say in a shaky voice, "Oh nothing, Sister. Mary is going to the toilet and she got really thirsty. I was just passing her a drink of water." Then I heard a knock on my stall. "Open this door immediately." There was no place to hide the fudge. As I opened the door, Sister's face turned blood red as she shouted, "Mary Murray, what is that in your hand?"

Dropping my head and my voice, I said, "Fudge."

"You were eating fudge in the toilet? Do you live in a barn? Does your mother feed you in your toilet at home? Do you know how filthy it is to eat in a restroom? I'm going to call your father and ask him why he hasn't taught you proper manners or hygiene. Now wash your hands and give me that candy. I'll dispose of it properly." My hope for a decent seventh-grade year with Sister Virgilia disappeared with that last piece of fudge.

And so here I was, a year later, at Sister Virgilia's mercy. I had no choice but to ask her a big favor. Red faced, I raised my hand and said, "Sister, may I please be excused?"

I think Sister saw the panic on my face and didn't ask any questions. "Yes, Mary, but don't be long. We're starting a new and important arithmetic unit this afternoon."

I tried to hold my chubby thighs together as I walked out of the room and took baby steps toward the girls' restroom. Thankfully it was just one classroom away. I ran into the stall. I had to tug my skirt and slip up and try to get my undies down without catching my underpants on my garter belt or hose.

Then I saw it—blood. I checked to see whether I had gotten

any red spots on my skirt, and breathed a sigh of relief to see my skirt was still clean. Thanks to Bertie's book, I sort of knew what was happening. But it didn't make me feel any better. I took toilet paper and folded it over and over and placed it in my undies and prayed. I walked back to my classroom very slowly so the toilet paper stayed in place. For the first time in my life, I was thankful for my chubby thighs. I sat in my seat trying not to move for the rest of the afternoon.

I couldn't wait to put my coat on and get home, where I headed directly upstairs to my bedroom. Tom and Bob were now away at college, so I finally had a bedroom all to myself. And their bedroom, which was now temporarily mine, even had a lock on the door. I needed privacy to figure out what to do next. I knew this was one of the taboo subjects, so I never even considered saying anything to Mom. It would just embarrass both of us. Maureen was never home, and she had lied to me the last time I asked her about the blood thing. So I couldn't ask her. I was on my own.

I had two lucky breaks. The room I inherited from my brothers had a small sink in the corner, and Tom had worked on the railroad the previous summer. He had a drawer filled with extra large red railroad hankies. They were cotton, soft, absorbent, and not in use at the moment. Just one, folded over several times and slipped into the crotch of my undies, did the job. I neatly folded two or three extras and found a small plastic bag to keep them in. I'd wash them as necessary in the small sink and hang them far back in the bedroom closet to dry. Each month I returned them to my brother's drawer and waited until the next month. And sure enough, as Bertie's book said, like clockwork, every twenty-eight days, out came the railroad hankies.

About a year later, almost to the day, I complained about my stomach hurting and I told Mom I was going to my room to lie down. She quietly came in and set a brown bag on the dresser.

"You are becoming a woman. You'll need these now. You can find more in the bottom cupboard in my clothes closet." That was the beginning and end of my sex education at 124.

OUR MAN-BOYS

It was the first week in May near the end of seventh grade. Spring had arrived, and the weather was warm and balmy. None of us wanted to sit in a desk all day. Sister Virgilia was beside herself trying to keep us engaged. Suddenly, she made an announcement. "We're going to change desks." We all loved changing desks. Our classroom was cramped, and our desks were close together. New seatmates were always welcome.

Most boys were still very young, but a number of mysterious boys had joined our sixth, seventh, and eighth-grade classes. No one ever said where they came from or why they were in our school, though there were whispers about problems at other schools or at home. We just knew they were older and they weren't Catholic. They were closer to men than boys—some even shaved. The man-boys were much more interesting than the boys we'd gone to school with since first grade. All the girls had crushes on them, and they all had a crush on Veronica Rizzo, the girl with the amazing breasts. In Sister Virgilia's seventh-grade class, our man-boy was Ronald Gray. He was tall, dark, and handsome. I mean movie star handsome.

So far that year, Sister Virgilia's desk changes had been carefully planned in advance. But since this was an act of sudden desperation, there was no seating plan. She announced that we'd be seated by size—the shortest in the front, the tallest ones in the back. We all stood at the front of the class as Sister went desk by desk, barking out names. I was among the tallest, so I ended up in the back row next to Ronald Gray.

I'd never had a real conversation with Ronald. He played on the basketball team, and when he'd jump to make a basket, we could see massive amounts of hair under his arms. We all thought he was a dreamboat. He was always nice, but quiet. He didn't flirt with or tease the girls.

Our desks were crammed together, and I wasn't sure exactly what to do with this man-boy almost right on top of me. I wished I'd stuck with my diet.

It didn't take long before Ronald and I started chatting and even giggling. He was fun, and finally, I relaxed. One really boring afternoon, while Sister Virgilia was talking about the importance of diagramming sentences correctly, Ronald reached under my desk and gently grabbed my hand. I almost lost it. Was it possible this handsome guy liked me? I was in heaven.

My fat butt and thighs were still a factor from my perspective, but they didn't seem to bother Ronald. I was sitting next to the best-looking boy alive, and he liked me, not Veronica Rizzo. At least I prayed he did. Our secret handholding went on for the next two weeks. I completely surrendered what little concentration I had and just basked in the love coming to me from under my desk.

On the last day of school, I was daydreaming about Berardi French fries, candy apples, and cotton candy. Patricia and I had laid out our plans for our annual best day of the year. It began with a sleepover at my house the night before our trip to Cedar Point for opening day. Bea, Bertie, Molly, and Jane were going to meet us at the dock before 8:30 to catch the first boat. In the middle of my daydream, Ronald slipped his hand under my desk and reached for my hand, but I was busy taking the brown paper wrappers off my books. Finding my hand busy, he put his hand on my thigh.

I stopped breathing. I thought I was going to faint. I could hear Sister Virgilia saying something about inspecting each book for any marks and leaving each in perfect condition for the next class. "Starting from the front of the class, take your books and place them carefully on the shelves under the windows."

I was paralyzed. I couldn't stand up, let alone walk. Fortunately, Ronald and I were in the very back, so I had time to try to start breathing again before it was our turn.

With that one move of Ronald's hand, my big first day at Cedar Point, Berardi French fries, and riding the tilt-a-whirl vanished from my mind. Whatever power Ronald Gray had in that hand was all I could think about.

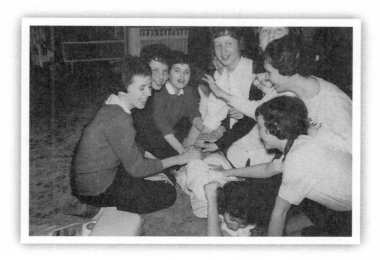

JESUS KNOCKS

Growing up at 124 East Madison Street didn't just prepare me for surprises, it also made me addicted to them. Mary Eileen Shufflin happened like that—a surprise.

I was in the eighth grade, and I'd been walking the halls of Saint Peter and Paul's for seven years. It was my second home, and this year it was finally all mine. No older siblings to tattle on me or embarrass me. My younger brother John Timmy was in kindergarten, but that didn't count. I adored him and wished I could see him every day and all the time.

I even had the beginning of real breasts. Things were good.

Sister Theodora, a seasoned and intelligent nun, was our teacher that year. She knew just how to give twelve-and thirteen-year-olds a long leash and when to rein us in.

On the first day of school, Sister had placed our names on our desks, and like an Easter egg hunt, we had to find our seat. I was hoping to be sitting next to Patricia, Molly, Bea, Jane, or Bertie. I was disappointed to find myself next to Mary Eileen Shufflin instead. Mary Eileen was from a family of seven, and her mom was in a wheelchair. I'd been in school with her since the first grade, and I liked her, but I hardly knew her, and she wasn't cool. We usually changed desks every six weeks, though, so I decided to make the best of it.

Mary Eileen looked just like me, except she had freckles. She was chubby and had a round face, everything I hated about myself. My mom and dad adored her. Whenever they saw her in church they would say, "Oh, that little Mary Eileen is so cute. She looks like she just got off the boat from Ireland. Bad break for a kid to get diabetes. It has to be so hard to be so young and not be allowed to ever eat candy." Everyone knew Mary Eileen ate gobs of candy, but I kept my mouth shut.

Not even a full day of eighth grade passed before I discovered a Mary Eileen I never knew. I already knew she was smart. She always won awards for the best everything that required brains. But I didn't know she was funny and daring. She made funny comments under her breath during class. I could hardly control my laughter.

The next day, a new young nun visited our classroom. "My name is Sister Austin," she told us. "I'll be teaching the fourth grade." She was petite with a high-pitched voice and a youthful energy. Except for her habit, she looked like one of us. She invited the girls to join the Saint Cecilia Choir. "Come to my classroom after school to learn more. We'll sing, but we'll also be a girls' club and have fun and parties together." She seemed to look right at me as she spoke. I was mesmerized by her.

Mary Eileen said, "Let's go there after school and see what it's like. It sounds like fun."

When we arrived at the fourth grade classroom, Sister Austin had her pitch pipe out and ready. We all tried to sing a few notes. I knew I was tone deaf, but Sister pretended not to notice. Jane and Bertie came too. Jane had a beautiful voice, and Sister was delighted with her. Carmen Caldrone came because among her long list of skills was playing the organ and the piano. The nuns loved Carmen.

The only requirement for the Saint Cecilia Club was to practice after school three days a week for an hour. Then we'd sing Friday night and Sunday afternoons at devotions. That sounded fine to me. I had nothing better to do.

A few weeks of choir practice with Sister Austin and doing homework with my new best friend Mary Eileen made me feel capable. I seldom, if ever, had to read out loud, and there were no more spelling bees. I was beginning to believe I was worthy and smart. Mary Eileen and I started hanging around Sister Austin and her classroom every day after school. We helped her do chores. She wasn't *holy* holy. She joked with us and encouraged us. We just loved her. Soon Sister Austin asked Mary Eileen and me to help clean the church on Saturdays. We didn't hesitate for a moment. If she had asked us to go to the moon, we would have agreed gladly.

★ ★ ★

I found myself torn between my two lives. I wanted to sleep over at Bea's house and go to the pizza parlor with Jane, get sodas at Fishers with Bertie, and party and shop with Patricia and Molly.

I had shared my life with these girls since I was five years old. They were my second family, and I adored each of them in a special, unique way.

One day Bea told me she was talking with Jimmy Stubbs every night on the phone. She said, "You should talk with him too. You will love his talking. He talks very soft and the words that come out of his mouth, I never heard before. You won't believe what he says. I keep wishing he would talk louder. I couldn't believe I was hearing right. You have to go with him so you can hear him." Bea was sweet and always willing to share with her friends.

Bea told Jimmy, "Call Mary Murray. She thinks you're cute, too, and would like to talk on the phone with you. Her number is 2665."

That night the phone rang. I grabbed it knowing who would be on the other end. I immediately took the phone into the pantry and shut the door as tightly as possible without cutting the cord.

I heard Jimmy in a soft voice say, "Sugar, your lips are like cherries. I would love to suck your big gorgeous red lips until they bleed. I can feel your hot breath on my neck. Sweetie pie, would you like to feel my hot breath on your neck? I want to caress your thighs and feel your warm body next to mine. Sugar, I want to bury my face in your sweet breasts. Can I put my lips on your neck and suck your beautiful tongue?" He never said my name or waited for an answer, not that I would have had one. He just continued nonstop. Finally, I could hear my sister outside the door listening to me. I would have to say, "Excuse me Jimmy, but my sister needs to use the phone." Then he would say, "Okay lover girl, hot lips, sugar . . . bye, baby."

Jimmy was a boy who never said one word in class. I think Sister thought he was mute. Well, we all did, until Bea discovered his tongue. He was good looking in a dark kind of way. He had black hair and the start of a black mustache, which at this point was just fuzz. He was tall but stooped over, and seemed painfully shy. I don't know what kind of a student he was, because he never talked. After a few nights of listening to Jimmy, I got bored. We stopped going together. I never saw him again after the eighth grade. I often wondered what became of him. I imagined him as a successful romance writer or the voice on 1-800-GotPorn.

I was the only girl Bea shared Jimmy with. Bea and I were in awe of his talent. After being under the watchful eyes of the nuns for eight years, he seemed like a wonder boy to us.

* * *

Shortly before Christmas that year, Sister Austin asked me if I'd ever considered becoming a nun. "Kiddo, you have just what Jesus needs to help him here on earth," she told me. I was shocked. Was she serious? Not me. Only the smart girls were invited to enter the convent, the girls the nuns asked to monitor the classroom, sell candy at recess, and help in the office. They were the girls who got perfect grades. But Sister Austin was serious. Jesus was calling me, and He didn't care one bit about my grades, or my thighs and my butt; he loved my soul. I knew my soul had to be much more attractive than my body.

"I believe you're being called, Mary. You must pray hard and listen for Jesus to whisper to you. He never shouts, he just nudges and invites." I would become a nun. Sister Austin and Jesus were giving me the personhood I was seeking.

Mary Eileen and I talked. We decided we would go to the convent together. We asked Sister Austin if we could go together to the motherhouse in Sylvania. Her response seemed a little vague but reassuring. "If Jesus is calling you both, then of course you'll both go. Pray hard, especially to Mary, His mother. She has very special powers."

Mary Eileen had developed diabetes two years earlier, and I was so jealous. Over the summer of its onset, she had lost about twenty-five pounds. But now she had gained most of the weight back, and she was chubby just like me.

Mary Eileen's dad, like mine, was always trying to make a little extra money to feed his brood. He made the most delicious fudge. It was milk chocolate—smooth and soft. I used to beg Mom to give me two dollars to buy Mr. Shufflin's fudge. She always gave in. She knew how hard financial times were for their family. Mom didn't know that Mary Eileen would sneak the fudge out of the house and pocket the two dollars for herself. After school we would go to Ohly's where she'd buy loads of candy and hide it in her school bag. We'd walk home munching on candy and talking about what wonderful nuns we'd be.

Sometimes we'd practice being nuns. We'd watch everything they did and imitate them. I'd try to walk quietly, projecting an aura of serenity. I'd laugh with a restrained trill and try to speak in a low, controlled tone. Then we would both burst out laughing until we almost wet our pants. We were going to be a different kind of nun.

Sister Austin gave us a list of clothing we'd need to enter the convent in June. It was a strange list. There were long cotton night-gowns, two black plain sweaters, cotton underpants, and cotton T-shirts. There were no bras. I had worked really hard to get my bra, and wasn't sure I was ready to give it up. But okay, for Jesus, what couldn't I do?

"This might be a good time to tell your family about your voca-tion," Sister said close to Christmas. "You can give your parents and your relatives this list. You can tell them these are the only gifts you'd like for Christmas, since you hope to join the convent in June. I'm sure they'll all be delighted and very proud of you."

I didn't give anyone the list, and neither did Mary Eileen. We both continued to clean the church, help the nuns after school, sing in the choir, attend choir practices, and do anything else the nuns asked of us. We planned our vocation together, but we only spoke of it to Sister Austin.

I tried very hard to be holy. I had started skipping breakfast before school so I could receive communion daily. Mary Eileen couldn't join me because of her diabetes; she needed to eat when she got up in the morning. I prayed a lot and I kept hoping I'd have a vision. Margaret Maguire had seen the statue of the Blessed Virgin cry. I stared and stared at the same statue, but not even one stray tear appeared. Mary Eileen didn't have any visions either, which made me feel better.

★ ★ ★

February was a bad month. Since the first grade, we'd started every school day with Mass at Saint Peter and Paul Church at 8:00 a.m. The Mass was in Latin, so it was really an act of discipline more than prayer.

On the morning of February 3, Bertie was almost late, which would have gotten her holy hell from the nuns. Bertie had a twin, Bobby, and they were both billboard darling. They looked like the Campbell soup kids, only cuter. Sniffling with her eyes all red, like she'd been crying, Bertie tried to whisper something to me, but each time she'd start crying even harder.

It was Sister Lorraine's day to patrol for misbehavior. Bertie always wore her coat slightly off her shoulders, so she provided a perfect target. Grabbing and almost ripping Bertie's coat off, she shout-whispered, "Straighten up this minute, girlie. Do you hear me? Get control of yourself, or you may leave God's house immediately. And Mary Murray will go with you."

After Mass, while we were walking to school two by two (and supposedly in perfect silence), Bertie finally choked out her news. "The Big Bopper, Ritchie Valens, and Buddy Holly were all killed in a plane crash last night in North Dakota." With that Bertie began to cry again, but this time really hard. Suddenly the other girls got the news, and they began to cry. I stood there, speechless. I didn't have a clue who they were talking about, but I was too embarrassed to admit it, so I just pretended to be sad too.

The next day Bea and Bertie brought their recordings of "Oh

Donna," "Peggy Sue," and "Chantilly Lace" to school, and we played the songs at lunchtime. The girls all fought back tears again as they mourned together.

Just a few days later, another tragedy hit. We learned that Eddie Fisher was divorcing Debbie Reynolds to marry Elizabeth Taylor. We had all seen *Tammy and the Bachelor*, and we were all Tammy in our dreams. We tried to wear our hair like Debbie Reynolds and rolled up our jeans to our calves just like Tammy. Eddie's move was a rejection of us, and everything we were about.

We'd all seen pictures of Elizabeth Taylor on billboards, advertising her movie *Cat on a Hot Tin Roof*. She was wearing nothing but her slip in the ads, and she looked really sexy. We were horrified that the sinful, impure, *divorced* Elizabeth Taylor had stolen Eddie from our Tammy. We hated her for life.

Now my focus was almost totally on Sister Austin, Mary Eileen, and my vocation. I didn't care about boys anymore. It was all about God now.

Mary Eileen Didn't Show Up

One cold Friday night in February, Mary Eileen and I chatted on the phone. We were doing a school project together, and we made plans to work on it the next day. We'd meet at the church for Mass, then we'd clean the church with the nuns, and finally head downtown to buy candy and go to the movies. After the movie, we'd go back to my house and work on our project. We'd cap off the day with dinner at the pizza parlor on Monroe Street, and then she'd sleep over at my house.

I waited in front of the church for Mary Eileen the next morning. Finally, as the bells were ringing, I went inside without her. I kept looking at the back door expecting my buddy to come rushing in, but Mary Eileen didn't show up at all that morning. It wasn't like her. It took me twice as long to clean the church without her, and it was no fun.

When I got home, I went right to the phone and called Mary Eileen's house. Her little brother Jimmy said, "Mary got the flu during the night and my dad took her to the hospital." That seemed strange. At least one person in my family had the flu almost all winter, but we never went to the hospital.

That evening my parents went out for dinner, something they almost never did. I was at home babysitting my brother. John Timmy was really more my pal than a babysitting job. I did the same things with him that I did with my girlfriends. We made French fries and drank Pepsi.

I knew our parents wouldn't be out late because Dad and John loved to watch *Gunsmoke* together. I wanted to call Mary Eileen and chat like I always did when I was bored. But since she wasn't home, I decided to call the hospital and check on her condition. I'd seen Dad make similar calls loads of times.

"Providence Hospital, how can I help you?" the operator asked.

"Could you please tell me the condition of Mary Eileen Shufflin?"

Without even a momentary pause, the operator replied, "Mary Eileen died an hour ago."

Died, died? This had to be a mistake. Mary Eileen and I were just starting to figure out how to live—and we planned to do that together, in the convent. My best friend could not be dead.

I tried to tell John, but he just looked at me with a blank look. He was only six. What context could he have for my tearful, "My friend is dead."

It was only a half hour before my mom and dad arrived home, but it seemed like forever. I ran out to the car as they pulled into the driveway. Before they were out of the car, I started to cry. "Dad, Dad, I called the hospital and asked the condition of Mary Eileen Shufflin. They said she's dead."

"Calm down, little girl, I'm sure this is a mistake," he told me. Like lightning he headed into the house, and Mom and I followed. As he called Providence Hospital I closed my eyes and prayed, "Oh please, God, let this be my stupid mistake. Please, please, please don't let my friend be dead."

Then I heard Dad say, "No, I don't believe it. What in God's name happened? She's just a child." The phone clinked down and Dad came over to me with tears in his eyes and hugged me like he was afraid I might disappear. Fighting back his own emotions, he held me so close I thought my ribs might break. I could smell his tar soap and feel his strong heartbeat. "I'm sorry, baby. Your friend is gone."

My mother put her arms around me and softly said, "Honey, I know this is hard for you to understand. But sometimes we lose the people we love. Mary Eileen is with God now. She is happy. Just trust God. He knows best."

A few minutes later, Dad said, "Give me Shufflins' phone number." Of course I knew it by heart. Dad called the Shufflins, and I heard him struggling to say, "Paul, this is Tom Murray. We just heard about your lovely little Mary Eileen. This is awful. Peggy and I were crazy about that kid. I'm so sorry for you and your family. If we can do anything, just let us know." After Dad hung up, he told us, "Seems that damn diabetes got her. They couldn't get her temperature under control. The poor kid went into a diabetic coma and just slipped away."

I wanted to shout, "We'd talked on the phone for an hour last night. Mary Eileen was going to sleep here tonight. She was going to the convent with me. We were going to be fabulous nuns together. How the heck do you 'just slip away' when you aren't even sick, and you're only thirteen years old?"

The next few days were a blur. Mom made the ham with the pineapple rings and maraschino cherries, and I baked chocolate chip cookies. Mom drove me to Shufflins' house to deliver the food. Margaret, Patricia, Jim, and Kathleen all greeted me as I walked in the door.

The little ones were all running around like they were having a great big party. Mrs. Shufflin was sitting in her wheelchair in the kitchen with Flory (almost two months) on her lap. Her steel gray hair was perfect, and her pale blue dress made her look like the virgin mother. She was placid, and didn't seem to notice the commotion of kids running all over the place. We made small talk that I struggled to get through. I wanted to go home and cry. I wanted to hate any God who thought this was a good idea.

Just before we left, Mrs. Shufflin said to her oldest son, John, "Go into Mary's bedroom and get Mary's little clip for Mary." He came out with a sweater clip that had Mary's name engraved on it. "I know Mary would want you to have something to remember her," Mrs. Shufflin said. "I hope you'll take this."

I said all the nice things I had been taught to say, and I didn't cry, not one tear.

On that short walk down the handicap ramp outside the Shufflins' house, I left behind my best friend, my dream, and my innocence. After that day, the world never looked quite the same to me. I learned to question God, but more than waiting for answers from Him, I think I just wanted to kill God.

Sister Austin tried to offer perspective. "Kiddo, God knows best. He wanted Mary Eileen to serve Him in heaven, and He wants you to serve him here on earth. Just trust God. He always knows best."

So I tried. I tried really hard. I sang in the choir and went to Mass and communion daily. I cleaned the church on Saturday and I hung onto Sister Austin for dear life. She'd tell me, "Your best friend is with Jesus. You can ask her to whisper your requests right into His ear. She'll be right next to you as you pursue your vocation. You'll still be doing it together. You are one lucky girl, kiddo. Few of us have a helper in heaven like you do."

But I couldn't help myself—no matter how hard I tried, I missed her. I missed her funny comments. I missed her brilliant brain. I missed doing our homework together. I missed how she made me feel that I was smart too. No matter how hard I tried, I didn't hear her whispering to me, and I couldn't feel her helping me from heaven. I just felt lost and alone.

MAY QUEEN

Each year, our school would elect a May Queen to crown the Blessed Virgin. It was the biggest event of the year. All we eighth-grade girls had to walk into each of the eight classrooms carrying our name in front of us. Children would cast a vote for their choice for May Queen.

Starting in the first grade, every girl dreamed of being the May Queen. She got to wear a white wedding dress and veil, usually borrowed from her mother. The stage of the gym was decorated like an altar, and a life-size statue of the Blessed Mother was on a pedestal in the center. The queen would walk down the aisle of the gym where the entire school was assembled along with any parents who could make it. The queen carried a crown of fresh flowers resting on a satin pillow. Her court of eight other girls, dressed in modest evening gowns with tiaras or flowers on their heads, would precede her. It was like being Miss America and a bride all at the same time.

I was chosen, and all the nuns said, "Mary, this is the greatest honor you can receive. The students voted for you, but they were guided by the Holy Spirit. For the rest of your life, you will need to live up to this honor." Sister Austin winked and said, "You had an unfair advantage, kiddo. Your pal in heaven was stuffing that ballot box."

Corso's Flower Shop was the most popular flower shop in town. We had three Corsos in our class, and one was even on the May Court. So the flowers were the best ever. Each girl had a bouquet of flowers to carry, and I had a crown of multicolored roses to place on the Virgin Mary's head. I wore my friend Patricia's sister's wedding dress and veil, which were much more elaborate than my mom's simple and understated post-Depression dress.

The procession started. All the children began singing as Sister began to play the piano.

> *Bring flow'rs of the fairest,*
> *Bring flow'rs of the rarest,*
> *From garden and woodland*
> *And hillside and vale;*
> *Our full hearts are swelling,*
> *Our glad voices telling*
> *The praise of the loveliest*
> *Rose of the vale.*

When we arrived on the stage, everything became silent. Then the piano and singing began again.

I walked slowly up to the satin pillow resting on the table and picked up the massive crown of roses. The children sang the chorus:

> *O Mary! we crown thee with blossoms today,*
> *Queen of the Angels,*

Queen of the May,
Of Mary! we crown thee with blossoms today,
Queen of the Angels,
Queen of the May

I slowly placed the crown of roses on the head of the Blessed Virgin.

It was the biggest day of my thirteen years, and I wished I could have shared it with Mary Eileen.

The school year was nearly over, and I was struggling to follow my vocation without my friend. Sister Austin kept asking me if I had told my mom about my plans. I had not.

One evening before the last day of school, I heard the phone ring. It was Sister Austin. She asked Mom to drive her to Toft's to buy some ice cream for the sisters. Dad had made it clear to the nuns years earlier that Mom was not available for driving or any other volunteer projects. She had enough to do running 124. So Mom wasn't happy when she got this call. She ran upstairs and changed her dress and put on lipstick.

I nervously rode along. Sister Austin and Sister Yvonne went into Toft's and bought ice cream and Mom drove them back to the convent. When we arrived Sister Austin said, "Mrs. Murray, I think I'll ride home with you. I need a little exercise. I'll walk back to the convent." I froze, knowing what was coming.

When Mom pulled up in front of our house, Sister said, "Mrs. Murray, may I talk to you for a few minutes?"

I jumped out of the car and ran into the house. I quickly put on my pajamas, got into bed, and pretended to be asleep. A short time later, Mom came into my room. Sitting down next to me on my bed, she said, "Your friend Sister Austin said you'd like to enter the convent. Is that true?"

Struggling to get it out, I finally said, "Yes."

"Your dad and I would be delighted if you decided to go to the convent and become a nun. However, you must finish high school before you make this decision. Then if you still feel the same way, we'll help you in every way we can." Mom kissed me and offered her usual, "Good night and God bless you."

That was the last word ever breathed at 124 East Madison about my vocation.

I spent that summer lost between Sister Austin and my promised marriage to Jesus, and preparing for high school.

I wrote endless letters to Sister Austin and waited every morning for the mailman to bring a response. Sister wrote that she was very busy taking summer classes. She wrote words of encouragement about my gifts and abilities. She said she could only write once a month because of her tight schedule, but she would see me in late August.

Then in late August, a letter came. It was postmarked Sylvania, and it was Sister Austin's writing. I headed to my brothers' room, the one with the lock, to read every word in private.

Dear Mary,

I have enjoyed all your letters and news about Sandusky. It sounds like you have had a very busy summer taking care of your brother John Tim and helping your mom and getting ready for high school.

I have my own news. I am being transferred to Cincinnati. I will be teaching the first grade. You know how much I love the little ones, so this will be my joy.

Stay close to Mary, kiddo. She will be your constant support. Remember you are named after her, which is a great honor.

*She will never let you down. And of course, Mary Eileen will
always be with you too.*

*Do not lose your vocation. I pray for you every day,
and will look forward to welcoming you into our convent
when you are ready.*

Come to visit me if you are anywhere near Cincinnati.

*Yours in Christ,
Sister Mary Austin*

And with that, my best friend was gone, Sister Austin was gone,
and my vocation was abandoned.

PART II
THE MIDDLE
1959–1966

SELF IMAGE

I had lived the last eight years wanting to be part of the big kids' action in my family. Finally, I had arrived. I was going to high school.

Except for the first two days of school, we were required to wear very boring and modest uniforms. All the Saint Peter and Paul's girls spent all of August 1959 searching for the perfect outfits for those two crucial days. We had a whole new group of kids to meet, and we were hoping to immediately establish ourselves as cool. Soon enough, we'd have to wear nasty navy blue jumpers every day.

I settled on two white blouses I thought would showcase my breasts. And I bought a beige skirt and a rose-colored skirt, which I hoped would shout, "This girl is not chubby, regardless of her thighs and butt."

I'd hated my body ever since our family friend, Dr. Joe Hertzberg, told me I was too fat. I was six years old, and was sitting on Aunt Sabina's lap while the adults chatted during his visit to our house. Aunt Sabina told me to pass the nuts around. As I was doing so, Dr. Hertzberg stopped me, but he wasn't looking at the nuts.

He said in a stern voice, "Come over here, little girl." Up to that point in my life, when someone discussed my looks, all I'd heard was, "Oh, those big blue eyes and that naturally curly hair—how beautiful." But then Dr. Hertzberg said, "Turn around." He took a big pinch of my butt between his fingers. He turned to my Aunt Sabina, who adored me, and talking as if I wasn't even present, he said, "This kid is too fat. What is wrong with Tom and Margaret? They should put her on a diet."

I tried to hold back my tears. Aunt Sabina immediately said, "Don't be silly, Joe. Mary is just right. She's big boned, but she isn't fat." Big boned! What the heck, how did I get big bones? I didn't even know what big bones meant, but I assumed they were like a dinosaur or a monster. From that day on, I hated my body, especially my butt.

★ ★ ★

I tried on my high-school outfits several times. I had on my beige straight skirt and popped into the kitchen to show Mom and Aunt Sabina, who was there chatting and having coffee while Mom folded laundry.

Aunt Sabina looked at me and said, "Turn around, toots." Aunt Sabina was unfailingly honest, and I could feel something was coming. Finally she said, "Marg, I think Mary needs a garment."

Mom, who was less worldly than Aunt Sabina, looked embarrassed, but agreed. I knew that "garment" meant a girdle, and I was amazed that they discussed this topic in front of me. But I didn't care—I was delighted. I was sure a girdle would make my thighs and butt look thinner. I lost no time securing one. I immediately handed Mom her pocketbook. She dug into her purse and handed me a ten-dollar bill. She instructed me to go to LaSalle's and ask the woman in the garment department to fit me properly.

I ran upstairs and jumped into my shorts and headed downtown to LaSalle's, which was only three blocks away. I didn't ask anyone to help me, though. I had been traumatized a few weeks earlier. Mrs. Miller, the woman who ran the teen department asked me if I would model for a little back-to-school show she was putting on. I agreed because I was sure no one would see me. However, the week of the show there was an article in the *Register*. Molly's mom saw it and told everyone.

Molly called and said, "Oh how exciting. You should be honored. We are all going to attend." It was too late there was nothing I could do but pray.

I didn't eat for three days before the show hoping I would lose weight. I didn't. The show was cheesy as I suspected it would be. Patricia, Molly, Louise, Bertie and Bea were all in the front row. I walked up and down the small runway wearing some cute clothes as Mrs. Miller described each dress. I took a deep sigh of relief when I stepped out to do my last runway walk. I even smiled at my friends this time. It was almost over.

Then Mrs. Miller said, "And for our grand finale, Mary Murray is wearing a dress from our brand new Chubbette Collection." All the girls, except Louise Brown, giggled softly. Louise burst out with the loudest laugh I had ever heard. I wanted to disappear into "thin" air.

So avoiding Mrs. Miller and the teen shop, I headed to the lingerie department. I picked out a panty girdle with long legs in the smallest size I could find. I hoped it would make me look thin. When I got home, I tried it on immediately. I could hardly walk, and breathing wasn't easy either, but I was sure I'd get used to it. Goodbye, butt and thighs.

And the miracle girdle worked. I wore the beige straight

skirt on the first day of school. I was seated in the front row of Miss Fievet's Latin I class. As she spoke to us in indecipherable Latin, I suddenly noticed a darling boy also sitting in the front row. His eyes met mine, and—wow. He was a Saint Mary's boy, and they were all new to the girls from Saint Peter and Paul's and Holy Angels. Already bored by Latin (but very interested in my new classmate), I suddenly heard Miss Fievet say, "Mary Murray, your job this semester will be to take the absentee slip and hang it outside the classroom door." She handed me a slip of paper.

I stood up and walked toward the door, sucking my stomach in and pulling my shoulders back. I had to walk right in front this cute boy coming and going. I could tell he liked me, and I offered a silent, "Thank you, God, for my girdle."

That boy's name was Larry Mueller. And that absentee slip changed my life. My plan to be a bride of Christ became ancient history. It was now all about Larry.

★ ★ ★

The Germans never said why Irish and Italian immigrants couldn't attend Saint Mary's School, but I guess they thought we could be a corrupting influence.

And they may have had a point.

The Saint Peter and Paul girls and the Holy Angel girls were fun loving and willing to bend the rules.

On the first day of class, Sister Marilyn, our very Germanic English teacher, said, "In order to get an A in this class, you will need to read six books and write six book reports every six weeks." She passed out a list of the books we were expected to read. They were all long.

I was now a pro at figuring out how to get around my reading issues. I knew I could never read a book a week, at least not if I was going to have all the fun I'd been planning on.

Molly, Patricia and I put our heads together over lunch. We decided we would start a book club. We had already become friends with Jacinta Kline and Krissy Bates from Holy Angels, so we asked them if they would like to join us. Louise Brown was a Saint Mary's girl, but we had already corrupted her (or maybe she had corrupted us). She was Molly's cousin and next door neighbor. We had hung out with her for years. She was a perfect fit for our book club, too.

The plan called for each of us to read one book and write a report on it, using six pages of carbon paper. We would then meet at 124 for book night.

We each passed out our book reports, which explained the main characters, plot, and so on. Then we went around the table and gave the story's details, including some small stuff to be sure we all had a handle on the story. Then we each wrote our own six reports.

We had created the forerunner to *Cliff's Notes*.

We all wrote great reports and got A's. And we had all improved our storytelling skills, which would come in very handy in the future.

Senior year, we restarted our club when Sister Delphine taught us history. On the first day of class, she picked up a huge textbook and said, "This semester, you will be responsible for every fact in this book."

Sister Delphine assigned a new chapter of the book every week. We had all heard about her class and my old book club was already prepared with carbon paper galore.

Sister Delphine sat behind her desk in the front corner of the classroom, often struggling to stay awake. She had each student's name written on a card. At the beginning of the class she would shuffle them like a Las Vegas card shark and in her deep manly voice say, "Okay, Larry, come up here. CUT." Then she would call a name, starting at the top.

That student would get up in front of the class and tell everyone what happened on the first page. Then she called the next name and that student said what happened on the next page. This went on for forty-five minutes a day, the whole year. Our club had our notes in front of us, so we would glance down at the upcoming pages while other students were presenting. And we all got A's.

If Sister Delphine liked you, she would stare at you when your card was next in line. Our book club was smart enough to make her like us lots.

After years of daily religious education, it never even entered our minds that there was anything wrong with our club. Actually, it was just the opposite. Sharing answers on tests or homework assignments was viewed as being kind and helpful. The nice, smart kids let everyone next to them and behind them see their answers. Some even whispered answers to help. It was our interpretation of faith, hope, and charity.

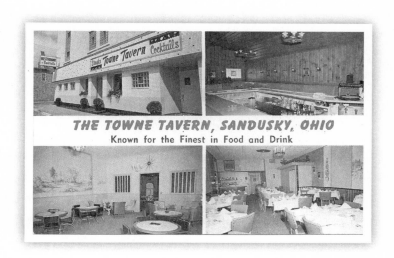

THE TOWNE TAVERN, SANDUSKY, OHIO
Known for the Finest in Food and Drink

DAD'S BIG IDEA

It was 1959. Dad had an idea: Sandusky needed a health club.

Dad owned a dilapidated building on Washington Street that had originally been a wrestling club but had been vacant for several years. "This will be the perfect location for my health club. Sandusky will thank me once this is open. People will pour in," Dad said.

Dad knew he didn't need an architect or a designer. Dad was sure he could do all those jobs better than any professional. We were familiar with Dad's perspective on such things. He was also a better gardener, plumber, electrician, and doctor than any professional.

Our kitchen table was not just for meals, doing homework, and coloring. It was also a procedure table when needed. We didn't need a doctor—Dad had a tool and a remedy for every ailment. The tool that looked like a small ax was employed for surgical tasks: removing verruca, boils, pus-filled pimples, and ingrown toenails. The kitchen table was also where ice was applied to bumps and bruises, and the occasional enema was administered.

When Dad was performing painful procedures he made more noise than a circus barker. "Now, little girl, this nasty little baby will no longer bother you. Say goodbye to this verruca. Oh my goodness! Look over there! I think I saw a bird. Or was that one of Santa's elves wandering around our yard?" Cutting, bleeding, screaming. "They're done. All done. Mommy, we need to find this brave little girl a treat." Out would come a Popsicle or a sucker.

Mom had her medical kit too. It was stocked with pink cures: Pepto-Bismol for stomach issues, Pinxav and Calamine lotion for skin rashes. No matter how much something hurt, it could be cured with a pink potion.

Murray fevers were treated with an aspirin crushed in a spoon and covered with Hershey's chocolate syrup. Miscellaneous diseases not cured by Pepto-Bismol or aspirin were treated with a tablespoon of whiskey with the alcohol burned out. (It was fun to watch the spoon start on fire.) And if all else failed, Epsom salts or Absorbine Jr. would cure whatever ailed you.

★ ★ ★

It really shouldn't have been a surprise when Dad decided to build a health club.

During the planning and building process, Dad reported his progress to Mom daily. There would be a sauna, dining area, workout room, a gym, and racquetball courts. But the best part was the massage room. A masseuse wasn't easy to find in Sandusky, but Dad found a guy who was legally blind and claimed to know how to give a great massage.

Dad went around town drumming up business. He offered free massages, discount memberships, and buy-one-get-one-free services. Business was slow, but then Dad had another idea.

Why not open the club to women a few mornings a week? They could have a sauna, a massage, and a bit of lunch with a friend, all right there.

This new idea was the beginning of my mortification and humiliation. Dad needed to hire a woman masseuse, also not easy to find in Sandusky. But Dad was always resourceful. He found a woman who was athletic and out of work, and decided she could be a masseuse in training. He would have the male masseuse train her for a few weeks until she had the techniques mastered. They just needed a guinea pig.

Since I was thirteen years old and a freshman in high school, apparently I was perfect for the unpaid guinea pig job. I was horrified. I cried. I begged. I pleaded, "Dad, please don't make me do this. I will be so embarrassed." And I cried and begged some more, unsuccessfully.

For two weeks, every night after school I walked downtown to the health club. I would take all my clothes off, wrap a towel around myself, and get up on a table. A man and a woman I had never seen before would touch, poke, and knead my fat thighs and plump bottom. I really thought I would never survive the humiliation. I told my friends I had a job at the health club after school. They thought that sounded cool. If they'd only known.

I tried to block out the horror of those sessions. By the time I arrived at the club, my stomach was so upset, it would be blown up like a balloon. The nuns drummed modesty into our heads daily for more than eight years. I had never been to a doctor or anywhere else where I had to take my clothes off in front of anyone. But I survived.

Actually, I survived better than the health club. It never really got off the ground as a business venture. It ended up being a great place for my brothers and their friends to work out and play basketball and racquetball.

I never went there again.

Fairytale Ending

We all had boyfriends but we seldom saw them. Most of us were not allowed to date, and no one could drive yet. Most nights in the winter of 1959–1960, our whole gang ice skated at Battery Park or sledded at Mills Creek Golf Course, which was across from our friend Krissy Burke's house. And we had slumber parties. Everyone bought new pajamas, and being included in these events was a huge deal.

Slumber parties were great at 124 because our living room was big and so was our kitchen. I only hosted a big sleepover if Dad was out of town. Mom was deaf, so we could stay up all night and make as much noise as we wanted. Mom always said, "You can have a party, but you must invite all the girls. I don't want anyone left out."

"All the girls" meant about sixteen. I convinced Mom that the really smart girls didn't want to come to my parties.

We giggled, talked about our teachers and of course boys. Mom would make a huge kettle of sloppy joes and a batch of brownies.

We had a real French fry machine, and everyone loved to make fries in the middle of the night and gobble them down with Pepsi. I could never imagine anything being more fun.

We didn't know it at the time, but our fairytale childhood was almost over. Many of us had no memory of life without each other. We had done everything together since we were five or six years old. Soon we would drive cars and have jobs, real dates, and real boyfriends. While we would stay friends, that safe feeling of knowing who you are and where you belong was going to change. We were growing up.

Modest, Pure, and Chaste

I had become a better student and was now an expert at covering up my reading issue. I loved to write stories, and that was the one thing I did well. Unfortunately, I still misspelled too many words, so that often affected my grades. I did well in math, typing, and even Latin and French. Most of those classes were just memorizing, and that was my strength. I still was uninspired, and found boys and slumber parties much more interesting than studying.

The nuns were determined not just to teach us, but also to protect our chastity. The last week of our freshman year, just before our first mixer, the time came for the Chastity Talk. The mixer was to be held in the gym at Holy Angel's Grade School.

Sister Generose taught us religion. She looked at least a hundred years old. My sister had told me all about her and how to get a good grade in her class. She had given Maureen a 140. 100 was perfect, but my sister did extra credit. She told Sister she said a rosary daily and wore the brown scapular. That's how she got the forty extra points.

Sister said, "Girls, please sit down quickly and quietly. No talking. We will open our conversation today with a prayer."

> *Dear Jesus, Lover of* chastity,
> *Mary my Mother most* pure,
> *and Joseph,* chaste *guardian of the Virgin,*
> *to you I come at this hour,*
> *begging you to plead with God for me.*
> *I earnestly wish to be* pure *in thought, word, and deed,*
> *in imitation of your own holy* purity.
>
> *Obtain for me, then,*
> *a deep sense of* modesty
> *which will be reflected in my external conduct.*
> *Protect my eyes*
> *from anything that might dim the luster of a heart*
> *that must mirror only Mary-like* purity.
>
> *Through Jesus,*
> *Fount of all* purity,
> *Amen.*

Sister ended with a dramatic sign of the cross.

We had heard those words—chastity, purity, and modesty—over and over for as long as I could remember. I wasn't sure if they all meant the same thing or something different. All I knew for sure was that we needed all three to go to heaven, and if we ever got close to the taboo "It," we would have the feared "mortal sin on our soul." And that meant an eternity in hell.

"Now girls, you are about to embark upon your first adult social event. Tomorrow evening, I want you all to have a lovely time, but to remember you are temples of the Holy Ghost. You want to keep yourself pure and chaste. You'll be representing your school, your church, and Jesus Christ Himself. People will judge our faith, our school, and your family based on your behavior. Catholic girls are always exuberant, but never immodest or boisterous.

"Always ask yourselves: How can I be sure my soul will not be marked with sin? Is my dress modest? Is my conduct chaste? Am I being careful not to be an occasion of sin for any young man? When I am dancing with a young man, is there room between us for the Holy Spirit?

"You do not want to give up an eternity of happiness in heaven with Jesus for an hour of pleasure.

"Cover your heads, girls. We will walk across the street to church quietly and orderly. Father will hear your confession, so you will take this step into adulthood with the grace of the sacrament to help you remain pure and chaste."

We all scrambled to get our mantillas out of our purses. Several girls had forgotten to bring a head covering. They tried to find a Kleenex to put on their heads and a few bobby pins to hold it on. The girls who didn't have either one resorted to the good-old bulletin. The church bulletins that were passed out every Sunday at Mass were always in the back of the church. If a girl wanted to enter church and didn't have a head covering, she could wear a bulletin on her head.

When we got to church, we had a long time to examine our consciences so we wouldn't hem and haw in the confessional and waste Father's time. After all, talking to the priest was really talking to God, since he was God's ordained representative on earth.

My biggest problem was coming up with adult sins to confess. I didn't want to rely on my childish standards of disobeying my parents or fighting with my sibling. I knew missing Mass, eating meat on Friday, having sex, or killing someone were mortal sins. I had never done any of these. My neighbor did kill his wife, but he wasn't Catholic, so he was going to hell anyway.

I wondered if my friend Sally would confess her sin. I assumed it was mortal. She didn't tell me, but I overheard her tell one of my friends that she thought she might be pregnant. She said, "My sister fixed me up with her boyfriend's brother on a blind date. He stuck his tongue down my throat when he kissed me goodnight. I stayed up all night brushing my teeth until my gums bled and gargling with mouthwash. Finally," she said, "I just decided to drink the whole bottle of Listerine." She looked as skinny as ever, so I assumed she wasn't pregnant.

Krissy Burke and Louise Brown were in the pew on either side of me. Louise kept watching how long everyone was in the confessional. She would whisper a funny comment if a girl was in the confessional for a really long time. "Now we know what she was doing at Battery Park last Saturday, ha ha." Battery Park was where everyone went after a date to "park and make out." Sometimes the whole place was filled with Saint Mary's kids. Many Catholic babies were conceived in that park.

Sister Generose had flunked Krissy in religion, so she was trying to act really holy whenever Sister was looking our direction. She had a rosary and would put her face in her hands and act like she was grieving, maybe even crying over her sins. Between the two of them, I was trying not to laugh out loud. It was almost impossible to focus on my sins.

The only sin I could think of was Larry. We'd been going steady since that fateful first day of Miss Fievet's Latin class. He was a farm boy, and the youngest in a big family, too. People said farm kids knew more about sex than city kids because they saw the animals doing it. But if Larry had learned anything from the animals, he didn't share his knowledge with me. He seemed to know even less than I did about sex.

Going steady wasn't allowed in our school, and certainly not in my home, especially for a thirteen-year-old girl. All going steady meant for us was seeing each other maybe two or three times a month at a party at someone's house—and, of course, saying, "We're going together." We never even talked on the phone because Larry had to do chores on the farm every evening.

Occasionally there were parties in the basement of someone's house. These kids had cool parents. My basement was a dungeon, and my parents didn't even pretend to be cool. Cool was like Mr. and Mrs. Arnold, my friend Margaret's parents, who wore jeans and khakis or sweatshirts and attended the school's football and basketball games. They were cool, but at the parties they were there—and I mean *there*. They'd pretend to pop in with chips and Cokes or cookies. We were visited at least every thirty minutes. The most we ever had the chance to do was dance to Bobby Vinton or Elvis and sneak a kiss behind the furnace or under the steps, if we were lucky.

Larry and I were like the blind leading the blind. We knew you were supposed to kiss if you were going steady, but that was the extent of our knowledge. Our kisses were so innocent that I'd be surprised if they even qualified as venial sins.

In eight months of going steady, I think Larry and I may have kissed twenty-five times, but I decided to say fifty in my pre-mixer confession. I wanted to be certain to say any sin I may have forgotten. I didn't want to die at seventy-five years old and find out I'd have to spend loads of time burning in purgatory for unforgiven kisses I forgot to confess sixty years earlier.

"Bless me father, for I have sinned. It has been one month since my last confession. I told ten lies (I upped that one too, just in case). I disobeyed my parents once, and I kissed my boyfriend fifty times. For these and all my sins I am heartily sorry."

There was a long silence. I worried that maybe the kissing was so bad Father would come out of the confessional and take me to Father Etzel, our principal. He may even call my parents and tell them what a slut they had reared. I wished I had started with confessing five kisses, or maybe even just one. Perhaps I should have explained that the kisses had happened over eight months. That wasn't much more than six kisses a month. Could that be a mortal sin?

Finally Father spoke up, "Dear, you must be very careful about these occasions of sin. They can lead to much more serious sins and loss of your chastity. Your purity is the greatest gift you can offer to Jesus and your future husband. And of course, dear, you don't want to be an occasion of sin for a young man, either. So when this temptation comes again, the two of you say a little prayer together. It is better for you to have fun with lots of different boys so you don't become too familiar with just one. Familiarity can lead to sin.

"For your penance, say ten Our Fathers, ten Hail Marys, and ten Glory Bes. Now say your act of contrition and pledge your heart to Jesus."

After the Chastity Talk and confession I still had no idea what sex or "going all the way" or "doing it" was all about. But I thought it must be amazing if I'd burn in hell for eternity for just trying it once.

★ ★ ★

I had worked hard to get to go to this mixer. My dad had decreed, "No dates and no boyfriends until you're sixteen." I thought if I asked Dad every day, he might get tired or distracted or forget that I was only fourteen and give in. And if that failed, I'd get Mom to intercede for me. That was one benefit of being the seventh child. You learned the tricks of the trade.

My brother Joe happened to overhear one of my pleas. "Mary,

come into the sunroom," he whispered. "I want to talk to you." Joe was always trying to help me. "Look, can you get me a date for that dance with one of your girlfriends?" Joe was a junior, and he was cute and popular. All the girls liked him. Getting him a date would be a snap.

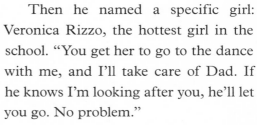

Then he named a specific girl: Veronica Rizzo, the hottest girl in the school. "You get her to go to the dance with me, and I'll take care of Dad. If he knows I'm looking after you, he'll let you go. No problem."

I talked to my girlfriend and told her my sad story. I needed her to help me get to the dance. She said, "No problem. I would love to go to the dance with your brother. He's really cute."

And Joe was right. Once he told Dad he would take me to the dance, Dad said I could go.

Larry and I didn't care how we got there, or who we went with. We were just glad we were going.

I saw a blue dress in a catalog and fell in love with it. It had a big bow on the back and a full crinoline-lined skirt. The top was fitted, which emphasized my positives. It cost $24.00. But I promised Mom to iron all summer to earn the money to pay for it. It was so beautiful I would have worked forever to get it. After all, it was my first dance.

The night of the dance, I stood at the door until Larry arrived to ensure there wouldn't be a single wrinkle anywhere on my beautiful blue dress.

Since Larry lived on a farm several miles out of town, his sister dropped him off at our house. He arrived with a corsage.

He pinned it on my dress just like a boy who had never done this before.

I was so glad Holy Angel's gym, the venue for the big dance, was only a five-minute drive. I felt so grown up and even pretty in my dress. I was officially going on my first date. I couldn't wait to walk into the dance hall and show off my dress and my newfound adult status.

Larry and I were sitting shyly in the backseat of Dad's Chrysler New Yorker holding hands when Joe pulled over and drove under the viaduct of the road. He turned the motor off, and he and his date disappeared from view.

Larry and I just sat there in an awkward silence that seemed endless. We had no idea what they were doing in the front seat, but the car was rocking up and down and breathing was heavy. Not a word was said. Larry and I tried to kiss. We knew we should probably be quiet, and I'm not sure what we would have talked about anyway. We even tried to get into it ourselves, but neither of us knew what to do. I twisted and turned and tried to sit on Larry's lap. It felt like we were doing gymnastics. I kept worrying about my dress. And the crinolines didn't allow us any body contact.

A half hour later, Joe and Veronica popped up like nothing had happened, and we drove silently to the dance.

The girl who'd been bouncing and rocking in the front seat looked perfect. Her dress was soft yellow chiffon and didn't have a wrinkle, and she didn't have a hair out of place. My new blue dress was a mass of wrinkles, my corsage was hanging off, and my hair looked like I had just been through a wind tunnel.

Larry and I had both been so traumatized we sat at the back of the gym all evening. Hardly a word passed between us. I wanted to disappear. I didn't want anyone to think I was a slut just because I looked like one.

DAD TALKED TO GOD

In the fall of 1960, a young Irishman, John F. Kennedy, was running for president of the United States against the man who had been Vice President for the past eight years, Richard Nixon. We referred to them as Jack or J.F.K. and Tricky Dick.

Dad, who was a lifelong Democrat, was over-the-top engaged with electing Kennedy. He couldn't say enough bad things about Nixon. "He is a goddamn crook, and everyone knows it." Dad couldn't believe an Irish Catholic could ever be president, but that didn't stop him from fighting for the cause.

Kennedy's opponents said that if he was elected, he would take his orders from the Pope, and the Pope would run the country. Jack Kennedy made a speech in Houston to a large group of ministers and said, "I believe in an America that is officially neither Catholic, Protestant, nor Jewish—where no public official either requests or accepts instructions on public policy from the Pope, the National Council of Churches, or any other ecclesiastical source—where no religious body seeks to impose its will directly or indirectly upon the general populace or the public acts of its officials—and where religious liberty is so indivisible that an act against one church is treated as an act against all." That ended the discussion. We were so proud that he was one of us.

An unusual sense of peace had overtaken 124 East Madison. Tom had graduated from Boston College and was in the army. Bob, Jim, Pat, and Maureen were all away at college. Joe was a senior in high school, and he was seldom home. He played basketball and baseball and always worked at least one part-time job. He was also the custodian for all of Dad's apartment houses. John, now seven, was still our beloved baby. Sibling squabbles and rivalry had stopped, at least from September to June. I loved it. There were only three of us sharing the bathroom, and we each had our own bedroom—at least during the school year.

One day, Joe and I were sitting at the kitchen table waiting for dinner and teasing John Timmy about having answered "48" for all forty-eight arithmetic questions on his test. John Timmy was clearly bored with school and decided to be creative. We said, "Hey, that's Dad's office phone number. Were you trying to call Dad, or do you just love that number?" We were laughing because John Tim wasn't phased by the zero sister gave him, or the note she sent home. We heard Dad's car screech into the driveway. Dad came into the kitchen all out of breath.

"Oh, hello dear," Mom said, standing in front of the stove heaping mashed potatoes and meatloaf onto our plates. "I bet you're starving. Let me finish feeding the kids and I'll make you something. I knew you'd be hungry and tired, so I defrosted a nice piece of sirloin steak. I'll get it going in a few minutes. How did your physical go?"

Two years earlier, when he'd turned fifty, Dad had gone to the Cleveland Clinic for an annual physical. Now, two years later, extraordinarily upbeat, Dad said, "Oh great. No problem. Well, a little problem, but nothing serious."

Mom dropped the serving spoon into the mashed potato pan and gave all her attention to Dad. "What little problem?"

Trying to sound matter of fact, Dad said, "Oh, they found a little spot on my left lung. I'm going back next week to have it removed."

Mom, always serene, said, "They're going to remove a spot from your lung?"

Dad laughed—not a real laugh, but the kind of laugh that attempts to cover up fear. "No, Peggy, they're going to remove the lung. Nothing to worry about! You only need one lung to live a full and active life. The doctor said I'll be hitting golf balls in a few weeks. The annoying part is that I'll have to stay in that damn hospital for at least a week, or so they seem to think. We'll see about that."

We were all thinking about Dad's sister Mary (Sister Jerome), who had lived her life as a nun and died from lung cancer ten years earlier, but no one mentioned it.

Mom dropped down on her chair at the kitchen table. Putting her head in her hands, she wept quietly. We never saw Mom cry. Joe, John, and I just sat, stunned, and silently watched.

Dad put his arms around Mom and said, "Peggy, my dear, dear Peggy. Now stop that right now. Trust me, this is no big deal." Crossing his middle finger over his index finger and flashing his steel-blue eyes toward heaven, Dad said, "The Man upstairs and I are like this. He and I have been working together for over fifty years. He didn't send me this brood of kids and expect me to quit before I finish my job."

Walking over to the table, Dad fondly tousled John's blond hair. "And finished means seeing this little guy right here graduate from college."

I wanted to cry and exclaim, "Daddy, you can't die. Who will keep me safe? I need you to help me finish growing up and go to college. I want you to meet my husband and tell me he's wonderful. I need you to walk me down the aisle, and hug my babies, and love them like you loved me. Please, oh please, Daddy, let me trust that you won't die." But I said nothing. I never wanted to make a fuss. So I sat silently and prayed.

I trusted my dad. He was the most honest person I ever knew. He prided himself in never lying to anyone, not ever. Dad said he wouldn't die, and that was good enough for me.

★ ★ ★

My mind flashed back to 1950 and the night a few weeks before my fifth birthday. It was less than a week before Christmas. I was already in bed when I was sure I saw a bad man on the porch attached to my bedroom, the room I shared with Maureen. I screamed, "Daddy, help me!"

Dad ran upstairs and swooped me up into his arms. I can still feel his arms around me. Dad wasn't a big man, but to me he was a giant. He carried me down the stairs and opened the front door. To my delight, there was a huge Styrofoam snowman on the front door. He said, "I hope you didn't wake up Mr. Snowman. He needs his sleep so he can make lots of snow for Santa's sleigh ride."

Then he closed the door and took me into the living room. Dad sat down and sat me on his lap. "Now tell me, little girl, what in the world could have possibly scared you?"

"I saw a bad man on the porch. He was really nasty looking and he said he was going to kill you."

"Oh, oh, sweetheart, there's no bad man on that porch, and why would anyone want to kill your dad?" he asked, taking his big white linen hankie out of his pocket and wiping my nose.

Sniffling back my tears, I said, "Because you're a lawyer."

Rubbing my back gently, Dad said, "Oh baby, no one wants to kill me. I'm a good lawyer. I get people out of trouble and help them. I don't hurt people or put them in jail. Now you listen to me. As long as I'm alive, I'll never let anything or anybody hurt you. So, little girl, back to bed now."

From that day on, I believed nothing could hurt me. I was safe as long as my dad was alive.

★ ★ ★

Dad once told me how I'd saved his life.

"One day I came home from the office. Money was tight, and my cases were slow and difficult. My clients were struggling and couldn't pay. I knew I was on the verge of a nervous breakdown. You, little girl, were just three years old, and you came to me so lovingly. You crawled up on my lap, and, putting your arms around me, you ran your fingers over the bristly shaved part of my neck. You always loved to feel those whiskers after I got a haircut. Your trusting little blue eyes looked right into my eyes, and you said, 'Daddy, I love you so much.'

"At that moment, I dropped my eyes and prayed that God would help me. I hugged you and got out of that chair and went upstairs to my bathroom. I filled the bathtub with boiling hot water and sat for a long time in that tub. I thought about you, my baby girl, and all my beautiful children. I told myself that I couldn't break down. When I got out of that tub, I was ready to go back and take on the world."

I hoped my faith might save Dad's life again. So I trusted him and I prayed.

★ ★ ★

A week later, Dad returned to the Cleveland Clinic and had his lung removed. I looked after John while Mom drove to Cleveland every day to see him. Mom was always home shortly after school, and had only good reports about Dad. She'd always end with, "But he's like a caged lion. You know how he hates hospitals."

On the fourth day, when I came in from school, there was Dad, walking around wearing his red velvet smoking jacket. He was shaved and looked like he'd just come home from his office. His chest was bandaged, but that was the only sign of his recent surgery.

The next day at school, Sister Bede, one of the grouchy nuns, stopped me in the hall. "Mary, what's this I heard about your father? Is it true he has lung cancer? What are they going to do about it?"

I laughed and told her, "Oh Sister, it was no big deal. My dad had a spot on his left lung. They removed the lung four days ago. He's already home and just fine."

She looked at me like I was a lunatic and she should do the world a favor and kill me right there in the hall. "Girlie, lung cancer is very serious. Most people don't survive that dreaded disease. You'll be lucky if your dad is alive a year from now. For some reason, you seem to think it's funny. I suggest you begin to pray very hard for your dad. I will ask Father to pray, too."

After lunch that day, a message came over the PA system. I heard Father say in a doom-and-gloom tone, "I would like to ask all of you to please pray for Thomas Murray. I just learned that Joe and Mary Murray's father is seriously ill."

I thought both he and Sister Bede were crazy. Dad promised he wouldn't die until John graduated from college. Dad never let me down. He'd walk me down the aisle at my wedding, just like he'd walked me into my first-grade classroom ten years earlier.

FROM HERE TO ETERNITY

In the summer of 1961, I was babysitting for the neighbors' kids and earning fifty cents an hour. My friend Patricia always had a real job. She was making a dollar an hour at the shoe store downtown.

The little kids I sat for had dumped their baby dolls and were now mad about Barbie dolls. The nuns told us this proved the devil was alive and well and prowling the earth to create sin.

I wasn't very interested in anything but boys, clothes, and who was getting their driver's license. I was fifteen that summer, but most of my friends had turned sixteen, or would soon. That sixteenth birthday meant a small two-by-three-inch card that would magically transform our lives forever. With our driver's license, we got our first real taste of freedom.

By then, I was dating the nicest and most popular boy in my class. Danny was the quarterback on St. Mary's football team. It didn't bother any of us that our football team hadn't won a game for as long as we could remember. It was our team, and they were our heroes.

Danny and I were going steady, angora yarn around the ring and all. Was I the luckiest girl in Sandusky? Yes, because Danny not only had his driver's license, but as an only child, he could get his Dad's car almost every night. Life couldn't have been better.

It was all so good. Danny was Catholic and had an Irish name, Kelly. Even better, my dad knew and liked his parents. My entire bedroom was decorated like a shrine to Danny, with pictures of him passing a football and playing basketball.

I still didn't know how a girl got pregnant.

I have no idea what my girlfriends knew or didn't know about sex. We actually never even said that word. It was considered dirty. We talked about everything (mostly boys), but "it" was one of those subjects we didn't discuss. We couldn't. If a girl knew anything based on experience and shared that knowledge, she was considered a slut. If she asked stupid questions that revealed her ignorance, she wasn't cool. None of us wanted to be condemned as either sluts or uncool, dumb little girls.

★ ★ ★

Even though my sister hated me, I adored her. Anything she did, I wanted to do, too. Whenever I copied her, she hated me even more, but I didn't care. I thought she walked on water.

A few years earlier, Maureen had worn a red and white Saint Philomena cord as a sign of purity. The red represented martyrdom, and the white, virginity. It was wool and she wore it around her waist covering her belly button. Even though I didn't know exactly what virginity was, I knew I wanted to be a virgin. I decided I would wear the cord, too.

It was itchy. Ever since our First Communion, most of us wore a brown scapular around our necks. That was itchy, too, but it was worth it. The Blessed Virgin herself had said, "Whoever dies wearing this scapular shall not suffer eternal fire."

As we got older, most of us pinned the scapular to our underpants, though the really holy girls put the itchy wool side next to their skin. I wanted to be holy, but that itching drove me crazy. I pinned mine on the outside of my undies.

Wearing both the scapular and the cord ensured two things: courageous chastity, and heaven. So it was hard to imagine ever taking either off.

One night in the summer of 1961 caused me a serious dilemma. Should I wear the cord and the scapular or should I take one or both off?

A bunch of us kids had snuck into the movie theater to see *From Here to Eternity*. It was an old movie, but we had heard it had the hottest sex you'd ever seen. We had to go.

Our parents didn't know. If they had, we never would have been allowed to see this movie. The *Catholic Chronicle* rated movies, and all our parents looked in the paper before allowing us to attend a movie. Any movie we wanted to see was rated at least B or C, which meant morally objectionable, so we rarely told our parents if we wanted to go to a movie.

We violated at least two commandments to see *From Here to Eternity*, the fourth and fifth commandments—we disobeyed, and we lied. These were just venial sins, so they were no big deal. In our hearts and souls, though, we were all going for the sixth commandment. This was the sin that created the mystery and the magic in our developing minds and bodies. We all knew for sure "doing it" was a mortal sin.

I hoped I wouldn't go to hell, and I didn't want to be an occasion of sin for Danny either. I wanted to be chaste, but like Saint

Augustine, I prayed, "Lord, make me chaste, but not yet."

My friend Jacinta (we called her Jesse) had been crazy about one of our classmates, Chuck, for over a year. Finally, one night at a party, he asked Jesse, "Would you like to take a walk with me?" We all knew this was the first step before you began dating. It was like a training run, a walk to a dark spot, the first kiss, and maybe a second or third.

After they returned from their walk and the boys left, Jesse, flashing her big doe eyes sweetly like only Jesse could do, shyly told us, "He kissed me." We all squealed. And Jesse continued, "I mean really, really kissed me. No one has ever kissed me like that before."

The next week, Chuck avoided Jesse. She kept trying to talk to him at lunch or in the halls between classes, but he refused to even look at her. She was crestfallen. After a week of ducking, Jesse finally cornered Chuck. He was embarrassed, and looking at the floor, he said, "I'm sorry, I can never see you again. I went to confession after our walk and Father said you are an occasion of sin. I could go to hell if I don't avoid your company."

Danny and I had been dating for over a year, and I was pretty sure we hadn't gotten even close to a mortal sin. But I was determined to figure this whole thing out. So a group of us told our parents we were going to *The Nun's Story* but instead we went to see Burt Lancaster and Deborah Kerr kiss on that beach. That was all the sex education I needed. Danny had the same reaction I did. The movie was all we could talk or think about.

A few days later, Dan said, "My aunt and uncle live on Rye Beach, which is very private. Aunt Helen and Uncle Joe always take a summer vacation." This summer, when they left, Danny had a plan. "You and I are going to spend every night on that beach, alone." Our teenage imaginations and hormones were raging. Finally Aunt Helen and Uncle Joe's vacation approached. It was a go.

My friends Molly and Louise (who lived next door to Molly) would help me with the logistics. Molly, who was dating Danny's best friend Don, would invite me to a sleepover at her house. She was the only girl in our class with a real family room, and it was huge. We had slept over in that room lots of nights. It even had a woodshed next to the fireplace that opened out to the back of the house. Some of the loose girls who were dating older, public school boys would crawl out of the woodshed and meet their boyfriends back in the woods. Those boys had cars, and sometimes these girls were gone for hours. We would all discuss and wonder what they were doing. No one knew, but we were all pretty sure they were committing mortal sins.

The plan was laid. Dan and I would wear our swimsuits under our clothes. I would take my little blue and white overnight case and a big blanket for my sleepover. My brother would drop me off at Molly's, and Dan would be waiting next door in Louise's driveway.

All went according to plan. I spent hours that day fixing my hair. I wanted to look just like Deborah Kerr. This was going to be my first big step into womanhood.

As soon as my brother Joe dropped me off, I ran across the yard to Danny, who was already waiting with the motor of his car running. We were both so scared we barely said hello. Danny headed right for Rye Beach. He parked his two-tone green Ford a couple blocks away from his aunt's house to be sure no one would see us or recognize his car.

We finally came to the entrance of the public beach. Then we had to crawl over lots of slippery seaweed-covered rocks to get to the private area. My freshly laundered white Bermuda shorts were covered in green slime. But we were finally at our dream-come-true beach. I could immediately see Dan was right. It was very private and very dark. There wasn't a star in the sky, and no moonlight. My blanket was really an old bedspread with football helmets on it that had been on my brother's bed. It was threadbare from washing, but big and soft, perfect for this occasion.

We laid the spread out neatly on the sand. Dan and I had never really been alone like this before. We were both shy. We turned our backs to each other as we slipped out of our clothes. That was the first moment I asked myself, "Mary Murray, what are you doing?"

Danny and I, now in our swimsuits, headed for the water. The beach was dirty and rocky and smelled like dead fish. The sun had gone down and, typical of Lake Erie, it had turned cool and windy and fast. As the clouds blackened, we both knew a storm was brewing.

No storm was going to stop us. We had planned this outing for weeks. We were going to be Burt Lancaster and Deborah Kerr.

The waves started kicking up and I was shivering. I jumped in the water to try to get warm and Dan followed. Soon the mosquitoes located us and started to buzz all around our heads. My careful hairdo went the first time I ducked under the water to escape the bugs. But every time I came up for air, the mosquitoes were waiting.

With my lips chattering, I said, "Hey Dan, let's just get out of this cold water and lie on the blanket."

I tried to run to the blanket just like Deborah Kerr in the movie. I sat down—more like a plunk, really—and tossed my head back. At this point Danny was supposed to fall down next to me and kiss me. And I was supposed to say, "Nobody ever kissed me the way you do."

But as I lay back on the blanket I screamed. It was covered with sand ants, and soon I was too. The wind had really kicked up now, and the sky was pitch black. Danny joined me on the blanket but instead of saying, "I never knew it could be like this," he said. "Let's get the heck out of here."

We grabbed our clothes and my football helmet blanket and tried to run back to Danny's car. We were soaking wet, covered in sand, and itching from insect bites. His car looked like Cinderella's carriage and I just wanted my prince to take me home. I wanted to see my mom. I wanted to bake cookies in my nice warm kitchen and go to my own bed. Alone.

Danny didn't make a fuss, but I could tell he was miserable too. My Saint Philomena cord and my brown scapular were sandy, wet, and itchy under my suit. They had done their job. My virginity was intact. Neither Danny nor I had managed even a venial sin.

THOU SHALT NOT

We returned to school a month later, and now we were juniors. There was a new urgency at St. Mary's about the taboo subject. Our principal, Father Lester, was serious and mean. He had arrived during our sophomore year, but it took us a little time to get to know him and his mission. We realized he'd been sent to ruin all our fun, and at the same time stop all of the out-of-wedlock babies at Saint Mary's High School.

There were too many senior girls in the last few classes who hadn't graduated because they were pregnant. The nuns and priests must have secretly freaked out. If they'd had job appraisals, they'd have been fired. Not only were there too many pregnancies, but also the percentage of St. Mary's girls was much higher than in the public school. That was clearly not good.

Father Lester announced a whole list of "thou shalt nots." No proms and no unsupervised parties. No one would be allowed to go steady. We were to socialize in groups only.

I was forbidden to be Danny's girlfriend anymore. The restrictions did nothing more than energize our loyalty and our hormones. Dan and I had never had a big love affair, but Father Lester gave our friendship new life. Just like Troy Donahue and Sandra Dee in *A Summer Place*, no one would break us up.

The boys were taken into a private room in the basement of the school for a one-day retreat with a priest from Toledo who wasn't really tuned in, but thought he was. After the retreat, we girls were waiting anxiously to hear what they learned. The boys wouldn't talk about it. The only hint we had was that whenever one of the boys wanted to get a laugh out of his buddies, he would shout, "Remember, no sucking tongue."

Nobody had a retreat for the girls, but we did have Sister Marietta who taught us health. There was one chapter titled "Reproduction." We were all anxious to see how sister would handle this subject. We had all read the chapter the first day the books were passed out. It was very vague. The drawings showed sperm and eggs and tubes and a uterus with a baby in it. It said something like "The male deposits his seeds into the female. The sperm searches for the egg inside the woman's womb. And if that sperm meets the egg, it is called fertilization and a baby starts to grow." That was about it.

Sister Marietta had a wart on the end of her tongue and she played with it constantly. It was very distracting, and it made her speech sound funny too. When we got to this chapter on reproduction, she said, "Girls, take your book home tonight and read the chapter on reproduction. There will be no test on this chapter. If you have any questions, ask your parents." That was the beginning and the end of our high school sex education.

★ ★ ★

Danny and I were really like old pals by now. He told me a lot of private stuff, like the very secret code for unlocking his front door. He told me what the guys thought about all the girls. I told him about the guys the girls liked and who they had crushes on. He told me what some of the boys' nicknames were—Kris Kringle, Polocat, the Stork, JC, and Tubby—and what they meant. I was only fifteen and didn't have a driver's license, but he even let me drive his car when he was at football practice. The only thing we never discussed was the taboo "IT."

One night when we were alone, I decided bravely to ask him about the boys' retreat.

I got him to tell me why the boys all laughed and pretended they were blind. Danny said that Father had told them, "If you enjoy touching yourself, you will commit a mortal sin. This is a very bad thing, and if you make a habit of it, you may even go blind." I hadn't a clue what that meant, so I decided to move on to the big question.

"Okay, did they tell you anything about, well, you know the S— subject? I know a guy puts his you-know-what in my belly button. But what happens next?"

Danny started to laugh hysterically. He really thought I was kidding. I wasn't.

I didn't expect this reaction, and I was embarrassed. I said, "What's so funny?"

Danny said, "Come on, you ARE joking." But then, realizing I wasn't joking, he said kindly, "You don't really think that, do you?"

I did, and we carried on a long conversation that included comments like: Want to bet? How do you know? Where did you learn that? Are you crazy? Finally, the light bulb went on. Utterly humiliated, I sighed, "Oh my gosh."

It was a rude awakening. I had really tried to figure it out. I'd considered all the possible places, and determined that an all-wise God wouldn't make babies where all that other stuff was going on. There was clearly disgusting stuff going on in that area. What was God thinking? I had a nice clean belly button, and that made a lot more sense to me. Not only that, I had worn that itchy Saint Philomena cord over my belly button to protect my virginity. Saint Philomena must have thought the same thing. I wondered if my sister knew the truth.

I made Danny promise he would never, ever for the rest of his life tell anyone my secret. I even made him say, "Mortal sin on my soul." It was the beginning of the end of our not-so-hot romance.

Danny did keep that promise. At least I think he did.

THE BISMARCK

The entire country was in a state of panic over the Cuban Missile crisis. Walter Cronkite reported daily on how our new young President Kennedy was dealing with Cuba and Khrushchev. We heard repeatedly how close our world was coming to annihilating itself.

Life at 124 East Madison continued to move and change. Another kid left for college every fall, and now John and I were the only full-time residents at home.

Dad loved cars almost as much as he loved the horse races and playing golf. When he saw the new Chrysler Imperial in summer 1962, it was love at first sight.

One bright sunny summer day, he pulled into the driveway like a kid with a new toy. He ran inside yelling, "Peggy! Peggy! Come outside and see what I bought for you."

Mom was accustomed to Dad's surprises. They'd been married more than twenty-five years by then. She knew there was never a dull moment when Dad was around. She calmly took off her apron and walked out the front door. There in the driveway sat a cobalt blue Chrysler Imperial. The taillights looked like red bombs.

Everyone in the neighborhood could hear Dad praising his new love. "Look at those tires, with the whitewalls and the spokes. Now, Peggy, that is style. This is the longest car in the USA. What a beauty. You deserve it, Mrs. Murray. You deserve nothing but the best."

Taking Mom's hand, Dad opened the passenger door and, pretending to be her chauffeur, said, "Aren't you the beautiful, talented Margaret Cummings Murray? Please enter my chariot. I am at your service."

Mom protested, "Wait, Tom, let me comb my hair and change my dress."

"Just let me take you for a short ride." Then he turned to me. "Mare, hop in, you can take a ride too."

I declined. I didn't want to be seen riding around town with my parents, especially in a car that caused everyone to turn and look. At sixteen, I knew that parents weren't cool—especially mine.

Baby John, now eight years old, was spending his annual day at Cedar Point with Aunt Lucille, so he wasn't around to take the maiden voyage of the Imperial either. The summers when Aunt Lucille wasn't in the mental institution, she'd take John to Cedar Point for a day. He would ride all the rides while she hit all the food stands. The last time they'd gone, she put him on the Ferris wheel, which was one of the highest in the world, and when John's swinging basket was at the very top, there was a mechanical problem and he was stuck up there for two hours.

"Didn't you and Aunt Lucille freak out?" I asked John.

"No. I just enjoyed watching all the excitement and the scenery. Aunt Lucille waved at me every few minutes and then headed to another food stand. I watched her eat French fries, cotton candy, a candy apple, a corn dog, and a milk shake."

By the time John and Lucille got back from Cedar Point, Dad

had come up with a grand plan—a car trip to a legal conference in Denver. He would attend the conference and they'd see the West along the way. "We'll visit Colorado Springs and maybe even stay at the Broadmoor. We may even go to Pikes Peak." Dad put his arms around Mom lovingly and said, "And I'll be driving you in the style you deserve, Mrs. Murray."

We all knew he didn't care about the legal conference. He just wanted an excuse to drive that marvelous car. Mom, as always, agreed to go. Trip planning took over the household buzz. Dad decided almost immediately who would go along.

John Timmy would go, of course, since he was only eight and too young to stay at home. Dad adored him, and would never plan a trip without his baby boy. Dad finally had the time to enjoy a child. He played golf with John. John went to Mexico with Mom and Dad. Dad even dressed John up in a fedora hat and a sports coat from his closet, gave him a half-smoked cigar, and snuck him into the racetrack.

Pat was almost twenty-two then and starting law school in the fall. "Pat, how would you like to be the only one in your law school class who has met and heard the famous Melvin Belli in person? You'll be way ahead of the game." Dad wasn't really asking. "You can help me drive if I get tired. How would you like that, my boy, driving a new Chrysler Imperial across the country?"

Maureen was twenty and super skinny from dieting. She had eaten nothing but tea and graham crackers for a month. Dad decided she would go, too. "I'll get Ennie trapped for a few weeks and shove food and ice cream into her. She won't be able to get away from me. You watch and see, Peggy. I'll put at least five pounds on that girl before the trip is over."

I was sixteen, and I was trying not to be noticed. I tried to avoid Dad. I thought if he didn't see me, he might forget about me and I'd be home free. I had fallen madly in love with a new boy. I was not leaving.

I was miserable. I talked to my boyfriend, who swore he would be true to me. I swore I would write him a letter every day. He said I was lucky to be able to see so much of America, and especially to be going in that amazing car, which I now hated.

Now I knew how my friend Molly felt every summer when her parents made her travel with them. We all consoled her and told her how mean we thought her parents were for insisting she see Europe. Who cared about Paris when it was summer and you were in love in Sandusky? Like Molly, I too would miss out on the beach, Cedar Point, and worst of all, the slumber parties.

Tony Sabino was my one true love. I had seen him on the steps in school the last week of my junior year. He was a year younger than I was, and handsome, but I'd never really noticed him. But that day, something happened. I guess it's called chemistry. All I knew was as he walked up those steps and I walked down, our eyes met, and my heart stopped. I was in love.

I pulled out my notebook and wrote my dear friend Susan

Schultz a note. Susan and I had been best friends since I sat next to her freshman year in Miss Fievet's Latin class. Susie was smart and fun. But most of all, she took care of me. She was like a mother, sister, and friend. She wasn't silly at all, but she allowed, and I thought, even enjoyed that part of me.

Susie never told me I was stupid or silly. However, she would say, "Do you think that's a good idea?" when she knew it wasn't. She saved me from doing a lot of dumb things.

> *Hi Susie:*
>
> *Oh my gosh! You won't believe what just happened to me. Just ten minutes ago, I fell in love, seriously in love. I need need need your help. Don't think I am stupid but you won't believe who I'm in love with, Tony Sabino. I have never even said one word to him, not ever in my whole life. I don't know what happened today. I just saw him as we were changing classes. His eyes met mine and I swear, it was love at first sight.*
>
> *What should I do? I can't just walk up to him and say "Hi, I fell in love with you today in the hall." I think he has been dating some girl for the last few years. I just don't know. Am I crazy? I seriously need your advice.*
>
> *Write back during French class. I am dying to hear from you.*
> *Me*

Susie wrote back.

> *Dear Mary,*
> *Oh dear. Sounds like you got it bad. What about Danny? You know he is the nicest and most popular guy in the class. The last two years you two were never apart. Have you*

thought about this?

I was sitting next to one of the twins in study hall. Not sure which one, but boy, they are cute guys. How come JC, Bob the dreamboat, and the twins never come to our parties? Would be fun if they did, but I think they think we are too silly and stupid. Can you blame them?

Miss Fievet is looking at me. Let's talk after class.
Susan

P.S. Did you see that skag sitting next to you in study hall? She had her collar up trying to hide what looked like at least ten hickies. Who is she dating, Count Dracula?

After convincing Susie that Danny and I were just great friends and he was more than bored with me and ready to move on, Susie agreed to help. Together we laid out a plan. She had never spoken to Tony Sabino either, but she agreed to be my matchmaker. She would figure out a way to approach Tony and report back.

Of course, it was awkward. I was a year older, and it would be humiliating to be rejected by a younger guy. I sat in study hall with my knees shaking and decided. I had never felt this feeling before, and I was going for it.

Susie cornered him in the cafeteria the next day during lunch. I watched through the crack in the locker-room door as they talked. Susie was no drama queen, and Tony was stoic, so I had no idea how her conversation was going. Finally, Susie got up, and, smiling, handed him a piece of paper. He wrote something on it. I thought that was a good sign.

The paper had the name and address of one of his friends who was having a party the day school let out, and he'd be there. He invited us to come. The kids there would all be a year younger, but my girlfriends and I were always willing to help each other in matters of love. Susie, Jessie, Krissy, and Patricia agreed to go with me.

Susie came over to help me get ready. She was encouraging. "I know he's going to fall head over heels for you. He sounded really interested."

When I walked into the basement party, my heart started pounding. I saw him standing there, staring at me. We lost no time. Within a few minutes, we were talking behind the furnace. After an hour of chatting, he asked me if I wanted to take a walk. He had no idea that I wanted to walk off the end of the earth with him. I was trying to be a seriously older mature girl. He was eight months younger than I was, and I was already sixteen and had my driver's license while he didn't. I was clearly the older woman.

We went on our walk. We stopped a few blocks away on a deserted street. He put his arms around my waist as we continued to talk. Then he brought his lips down to mine. I pulled back quickly and said, "I'm sorry, I never kiss on the first date." My sister taught me that one. She said that's how she got her boyfriend to fall in love with her.

"You need to make it clear you aren't a slut, you're a good girl," Maureen had advised.

My heart sunk when I said it, though. I wanted to say, "Kiss me, kiss me, rip my clothes off and take my chastity, virginity, modesty, purity." I was ready for mortal sin that night.

Tony looked embarrassed and said, "Oh, I'm sorry. I'm really sorry. Could we go out tomorrow night?" I could hardly breathe. It worked.

And that's how it began. I was sure I was going to be Mrs. Tony Sabino. Except now, only six weeks into the love affair of my life, Dad wanted me to go away for two weeks. That sounded like forever. What if Tony found someone else while I was away?

I tried to get out of it, but Dad was way too smart to allow a sixteen-year-old with raging hormones and an Italian boyfriend to stay home alone. "Marzie, you're going, and that's it. You'll see the country and have a great time."

So the trip was on. Pat, Maureen, and I would ride in the back-seat. John, Mom, and Dad would ride in the front.

★ ★ ★

I didn't know whether Iowa and Nebraska actually covered half of the U.S., but it sure felt like it. For most of the trip, there was nothing to see but cornfields. It didn't take long before we began to realize this trip would be very long. We were constantly looking for someplace to stop. Finally Dad would pull off the road and send us all into the fields to pee. When and if we saw a restaurant, we stopped and ate regardless of how awful it looked—and most looked awful. We'd know whether Mom thought a restaurant had questionable hygiene if she ordered a hamburger. "Can't do much to ruin hamburger," she'd say.

On the third day, Dad was trying to make it to the next gas station. "We're flying on fumes," he kept shouting. There hadn't been a gas station for what seemed like hours. Suddenly the sky turned pitch black and we realized we were driving into a huge storm. The wind picked up and rain and hail came down faster and harder than I had ever seen. Dad pulled off the road onto the shoulder of the road, and as he did the windows of the Imperial started to leak and water poured in. "Son of a bitch, cover the windows," Dad yelled. "That horse's ass John Gaking. I'm going to sue his ass when I get home. This is the last car I'll ever buy from him."

Mom calmly reached in the backseat and got some paper cups.

She handed some to each of us and we sat holding the cups up to the windows until the storm passed and the sun popped out.

Soaking wet, we finally reached a small town with a gas station and a restaurant that looked really nice. Dad whipped into the parking lot, and Mom told us to go to the restrooms and get as many paper towels as we could find. We did our best to dry the car and ourselves up. And our reward was to be a nice, quiet dinner. We were all starving, and this was our first nice restaurant on the road. Mom even ordered spaghetti instead of a hamburger.

I always ordered spaghetti. It had been my favorite dinner since I was a little girl. Once a month, Dad would take us all to the IAB club (Italian American Brotherhood) for dinner. That is where I learned to love spaghetti. I loved it so much, my family had said for years, "Mary has a little Italian in her." But this night, Pat, trying to tease me said, "I think Marzie has a little Italian in her." Dad glared at me over his glasses and said, "She damn well better not."

Dad was enjoying a nice bottle of Heineken in between rages about his new car. We were finally dry after the afternoon deluge, and the food was really good. Suddenly, interrupting our first brief moment of comfort, a huge bat swooped down and flew right across our table. Maureen screamed as it grazed her head.

Dad yelled, "Goddammit, Maureen. Be quiet." Then, jumping up from the table, he took his jacket off and, swinging his jacket up and down, he darted around the restaurant, screaming, "You son of a bitch. You met your match in T. J. Murray."

Mom calmly turned to Maureen and me and said, "Put your napkin on your head. Bats go for your hair." So the three Murray women sat there with napkins on our heads. John Timmy, who never knew life without madness, seemed unfazed. Dad's bat hunts were familiar to us all.

Everyone else in the restaurant just sat there, shocked. Dad was knocking over chairs, hitting people and plates of food with his jacket. Spaghetti, French fries, and bread were flying around as Dad jumped and ducked and shouted at the bat, "You little son of a bitch. I'll get you, you bastard."

Suddenly, and without a word, Pat got up from our table and walked over to the door. He opened it and the bat flew out, inspiring cheers from the other diners.

Back on the road, Mom turned to Dad and said, "Tom, did you enjoy your dinner? My spaghetti was delicious. I hope you enjoyed yours. What do you think, kids? Wasn't dinner great?"

We finally arrived in Denver and the four of us kids were together now for almost five days—and I mean together. Pat and John slept in one double bed, and Maureen and I in the other. Pat, who'd always been beyond modest, was disgusted to be sharing a room with his sisters.

Just one day into the conference, Dad announced, "That Melvin Belli is a bag of wind. That fat ass doesn't know a thing about the law. We're going to Colorado Springs tomorrow morning."

None of us were happy to be getting in the car again, but the next morning we were off. I begged Dad to just take us home. Pat teased, "Oh, Marzie is in love. She can't live without her Italian lover boy."

We arrived in Colorado Springs before lunch. Dad was like an excited kid. He said, "We're going to have lunch at the Broadmoor today." We drove up to the hotel and it looked fabulous. There was even a giant swimming pool. We were all dreaming of spending a few days there, as Dad had promised.

Instead of pulling up in front of the hotel, though, Dad drove two blocks away and parked the car on the street. "Now you all just wait here. I'm going up to the hotel to negotiate a rate for two rooms for two nights. I don't want them to see this car. They'll think we're loaded, and may try to soak me."

In less than fifteen minutes, we saw Dad coming back looking dejected. He got in the car and turned to Mom. "Those thieves. You wouldn't believe how much they wanted for a room. It would have been over three hundred dollars a night for all of us to stay here. We'll find somewhere else nice and drive up to Pikes Peak."

In all, we were gone for two weeks. Before we returned home we had stayed in a hut on sticks that required a climb up a ladder to get into it. We stayed in a cabin with no electricity and another with an outhouse. We had eaten in greasy spoons across Wisconsin, Iowa, Nebraska, and Colorado. Mom had eaten a lot of hamburgers.

MAUREEN IN LOVE

It was May of 1963. I was a month away from graduating high school, and Maureen was in love. I'd been in love nonstop since I was twelve. As Pat liked to say, "Marzie is in love with love." But this was a first for Maureen, and it made her much nicer. She wasn't engaged, but her boyfriend, Mike, was visiting all the time, and she was clearly gaga about him. Her lover boy was Hungarian, and he loved good food, and lots of it.

Mike had been around enough to know what a crazy place 124 was, so little surprised him. His inaugural visit was Thanksgiving 1960. And Thanksgivings were always interesting at 124.

I could hear Dad shouting on the phone. "Stop right now, little girl, and listen to me. You will be driving right past the goddamn hospital. It will be no trouble for you to stop. And it will be a big help to me. I called Lucille's doctor earlier today and it's all arranged. You'll have no trouble getting into the hospital. They'll be looking for you. If that boyfriend of yours needs directions, tell him to call me."

I could hear Maureen sobbing on the phone. She was hysterical, but that wasn't unusual. Hysteria was Maureen's normal reaction. Dad called her his "harlequin."

"No, please Dad, no. Can't someone else pick up Aunt Lucille? Why can't Bob or Joe do it? You don't understand. I really like this guy. He doesn't even know I have an aunt in a mental institution. What will he think about me and our family?"

Maureen was going to stop on her way home from college at the infamous Toledo State Mental Hospital to pick up Aunt Lucille for Thanksgiving dinner at our home. She would spend the weekend with Aunt Sabina, and Maureen would take her back on Sunday. There would be no more discussion.

I had dreamed about my older siblings bringing girlfriends and boyfriends home, just like in the movies. I was really anxious for Maureen to arrive home. It was her first time home since going to college, and she had a boyfriend. I knew she would be nice to me in front of her lover boy.

The night before Thanksgiving was now better than ever. Most of my siblings would be arriving, and the house would be bustling again. Since it was only four days, we could all stand each other.

We were used to playing musical beds. Mom always figured out how to juggle bedrooms to accommodate extra kids. She put Maureen's boyfriend, Mike, in Tom's bedroom. Jim was at Boston College, which was too far to make it home for just the weekend, so there would be a spare bed.

When Maureen hit the front door, it all started to happen again. Aunt Lucille was cheerful as always, and Maureen was hysterical. Aunt Lucille had gotten into the backseat of Mike's sacred black convertible and plunked down on the box of two dozen eggs Maureen had brought with her. Lucille hadn't noticed that she was sitting in scrambled eggs until they pulled into 124.

★ ★ ★

Until Mike appeared, Maureen had hated anything to do with the kitchen, including eating. She inspired the expression "She doesn't know how to boil water."

Maureen asked me to teach her how to cook and bake. It had to be a crash course. She had to get good, and fast. Mike's mother had told him not to marry Maureen. "She's a china doll," she said. "And china dolls are nice to look at, but they are not for marrying. If you marry this girl from an Irish home, you will eat nothing but beans and wieners every day."

It was true. Maureen was petite and beautiful, with lovely, delicate features and big blue eyes. And she couldn't cook. And she did love beans and wieners, even though she didn't know how to cook them.

Maureen decided her first step toward becoming Julia Child and winning over Mrs. Gergely should be a baby step. She would make chocolate chip cookies. I got the bag of Toll House chocolate chips and went through the directions with her. I even pulled out the cookie sheet and the Crisco lard for greasing the pan.

Maureen decided her maiden bake-off deserved an audience. "Call your boyfriend and tell him I'm going to make chocolate chip cookies tomorrow. He should come home with you right after school if he wants warm cookies right out of the oven."

When Tony Sabino and I opened the front door the following afternoon, the heavenly aroma of cookies baking hit us right in the face. Maureen stood in the kitchen proudly wearing one of Mom's cobbler aprons and hot gloves. She had already poured two big glasses of milk for us when the buzzer on the oven trumpeted.

She opened the oven door and pulled out the cookie sheet. She put it on the kitchen table and just stood there looking stunned.

There was a cookie, but only one, and it looked like a domed roof. It covered the entire pan and was about six inches high in the middle.

Maureen, almost crying, said, "What happened?"

I was trying not to laugh because I could see that she didn't find it funny. Every time Tony tried to pick up a hunk of cookie, it would crumble in his hand. He kept trying to munch on scraps and kept saying, "Don't worry, I love these cookies. They taste really good."

Suddenly I noticed the Bisquick box sitting on the counter. Picking it up, I asked, "Maureen, you didn't use this, did you?"

Now annoyed, she said, "You said to use two and a half cups of flour."

Clearly we had lots more work to do before Maureen could show off her culinary prowess to Mike and his mother.

★ ★ ★

When the Town Club didn't take off, Dad had another dream. He loved eating and being where the action was. He always said, "Sandusky needs a really good first-rate restaurant. It's a shame you have to drive all the way to Cleveland to get a good meal."

So Dad decided *he* would be the person to open the first five-star restaurant in town.

The building that housed the Town Club had a large, street-level area that would be perfect for Dad's restaurant. For weeks, he talked about the name. He came up with an endless array of names.

Dad would say, "Peggy, what do you think of this? Washington Street Inn. The Town Roadhouse. Better yet . . . Murray's Pub? No, no. Not good." Finally, one night at dinner, Dad shouted, "Peggy, I've got it! I just came up with the perfect name. We'll call it The Town Tavern." Mom didn't say anything. She knew by the tone of Dad's voice that he had fallen in love with this name.

Next, Dad designed the cocktail lounge, the restaurant, the bar, and the menu. "We'll have an elegant room where the ladies can have daiquiris, whiskey sours, or gimlets, and the men can have martinis and Manhattans. We'll have the best filet mignon, but also lobster tails and live lobsters—and fresh Lake Erie perch. And it will be elegant, but warm and inviting."

Dad was a lawyer, not a designer or restaurateur, but that never bothered him one bit. "I know good food, and I know what people like. They will be lined up to eat at THE Town Tavern. Who knows, maybe when they eat in the restaurant, they'll want to join the Town Club."

And this time, one of Dad's dreams really made it.

The Town Tavern would have a T. J. Murray–designed interior. It would serve the best food for miles around. Al Hosfeldt and his wife had been manager at Plum Brook Country Club, and Dad loved them both. "That little wife will manage the place beautifully, and Al knows good food and how to make it." And having his dear friends running the restaurant would allow Dad to give endless opinions about how to make it the best place in Ohio.

The restaurant occupied most of the conversation at 124 for at least a year. And Dad was in his glory. "Peggy, we added tenderloin tips to the menu, and they melt in your mouth."

Dad loved owning a restaurant. Mom and Dad took John there almost every weekend for dinner. Dad ate lunch there most days. It also provided summer and holiday jobs for all my brothers, who bussed and waited tables.

Dad wouldn't allow Maureen or me to work in the restaurant. That was not ladylike. Dad gave me a small job appropriate for a girl. He told me to show one of his apartments to a couple who had called in response to an ad he had placed in the paper. He said, "Marzie, this will be good for you—good experience." He gave me the keys and, grabbing the keys to Mom's Nash Rambler, I headed to the apartment building.

An hour later I came home. Plopping the $50.00 cash deposit into Dad's hands, I said, "I was successful. They want to rent for at least one year, maybe two. They will stop by your office this afternoon to sign the contract."

I felt very grown up and important, and Dad was delighted. "Okay, that's my girl." I loved working at Cedar Point, but I now imagined a big sales job in my future.

Two hours later Dad came in the door laughing so loud that everyone came to see what was so funny. Dad shouted, "Where's Marzie?" I came running down the stairs, hoping to get more praise and maybe a tip.

Instead, Dad said, "Little girl, do you know who you rented the apartment to this morning? They were a couple of hillbillies, and get this, Peggy—they aren't married. Of course I gave them their deposit back, and told them no honest landlord in town will rent to them unless they're married."

At my age, I just wanted to be like everyone else. My father always embarrassed me. And he made it pretty easy to be embarrassed.

If I went to The Town Tavern with Mom, Dad, and John, Dad would spend the whole evening stopping at every table, asking, "How do you like those frog legs? Have you tried our live lobsters yet? We're famous for our garlic bread. Try some—you'll love it. Best prime rib in the country." When Dad asked, "How do you like something?" he never waited for an answer, he just raved about the food himself.

But the worst part was Dad's decision to purchase a motorized surrey with a fringe on top. He said excitedly, "This will be a fun way to advertise the restaurant." He put a big sign on the side of the surrey that read "The Town Tavern. THE Place to Meet &

Eat." He wanted me to drive it all around town wearing a big hat and tooting the horn, waving as I drove all over. At sixteen, I was not about to call that kind of attention to myself.

On Maureen's wedding day, Dad even made her get in the surrey and drive down Columbus Avenue with her husband in her wedding dress.

Thankfully, by the time the restaurant was in full swing, I was working at J.C. Penney's and Cedar Point, so I was able to duck and run. But occasionally I did have to witness one of Dad's daily drives.

FAREWELL TO 124

In the fall of 1963, I entered college in somewhat the same way I entered the first grade. Sure, this time I had some warning. But just like that morning when my father dragged me unceremoniously into Sister Lorraine's classroom, I knew I didn't belong.

While I was worrying about college, we got some big news. Tom (who was in law school at the University of Virginia) called to announce his engagement to Ann Leitch. None of us had ever even heard her name. But that was Tom—he lived in his own world, and only occasionally allowed us in.

Ann was a senior at the University of Virginia. Tom told Mom, "Ann is the smartest lady I've ever met. She is brilliant, refined, and a daily communicant. I'm bringing her home over Labor Day weekend to meet the family. I would appreciate it if everyone would behave well and not embarrass me." Being the oldest, Tom never asked, he told. That's how he'd earned his nickname: The Bully. He wasn't mean, though. He didn't have to be, he always got his way.

Mom began to worry immediately. She started to pick at her fingernails, which was the only evidence we ever had that she was nervous. Where would she put this southern lady? Mom was used to boys in the house. My brothers brought roommates or guy friends home regularly, and Maureen had her boyfriend Mike there all the time. But a girl was different, and such a refined girl was intimidating. Even everyday events could cause trauma at 124, so the first son to bring a bride-to-be home was sure to cause ripples.

I was more concerned about getting to college than how Tom's meet-the-family would go. Child number seven leaving for college was no big deal. Dad adored me. I was his baby girl. But he was not taking me to college. That possibility never would have entered his mind, or mine for that matter. I had done a great job of learning how to fly under the radar. The last thing I wanted or needed was for Dad to start taking an interest in my personal life.

Dad had strong views about some of the milestones in our education lives. Well before it was my turn, for example, Dad had decided not to attend our graduation ceremonies. He had attended Tom's graduation from Sandusky High School. He'd had his fill. "What's the big deal?" he'd ask each spring. "Every moron graduates from high school these days. It's that goddamn Spock who makes these kids all feel like little pieces of importance. High school, what a joke." And after he attended a couple of college graduations, he offered, "What's the big deal? Anyone who has a father paying for his education can and should graduate from college. The world is full of morons who graduated from college. I'll wait and see if any of these kids learned anything, like how to work. Then I'll celebrate with them." And so, amen to graduations.

My dorm at the University of Dayton, Marycrest Hall, would open the day after Labor Day, and orientation began the next day. The weeks were passing, and I needed to figure out how I was going to get to campus. Mom said I could take a Greyhound bus, but I had my radio and clothes, and even a metal box filled with winter clothes to store under my bed. I couldn't take all that on the bus, and I couldn't go to college without my stuff.

Joe stepped in to help. He was going to be a junior at the University of Dayton, and Dad had given him his old Chrysler. "I can take Mary to Dayton. The only problem is that I start ROTC and my job at J.C. Penney's four days before school starts." Joe was living off campus in a fraternity house with a bunch of guys. He was a big man on campus. "Don't worry, though, I can arrange it all for you." That should have sparked a memory of Joe's "arrangement" of my memorable first date, during which Larry and I sat awkwardly in the backseat while Joe and his date set the car rocking in the front seat. But it didn't.

Joe made a few phone calls, and the plan was made. One of his priest friends at the university agreed to give me a key to the dorm. Everyone was happy. My slightly earlier departure solved the bed shortage problem during Tom and Ann's visit, and I had transportation to college. Mom relaxed a little.

I didn't consider how lonely and scary it would be to stay alone in Marycrest Hall, an eight-story building meant to house four hundred girls. I was the only person in the entire building for four days and four nights. There was nothing open on campus, so I just ate the chocolate chip cookies I had brought with me, and cried. I unpacked and organized the room. I tried to read, but I heard noises. I tried to write letters to all my girlfriends, but there wasn't much to say. This was not how I had imagined college.

★ ★ ★

Leaving home with a broken heart probably added to my sadness. A few weeks before my departure, Tony Sabino (the love of my life) called and sweetly invited me out for a going-away dinner. I laughed and said, "Isn't this a little early? I'm not leaving for almost four weeks." He didn't laugh.

I loved going anywhere with him, but I especially liked going to adult restaurants. He'd been working a part-time job for years, and he was always generous, buying me gifts and entertaining me at lovely places. He had given me a charm bracelet for Christmas, and every month that followed, he surprised me with a new charm to celebrate our monthly anniversary. There was a heart, a cross, a shamrock, and a charm saying "NO." We had celebrated our first anniversary with a fancy dinner at The Stone House. That night he gave me a silver charm shaped like a record. It was engraved with "A Date to Remember, 6-8-1962," the night of our first date.

We had talked all summer about my going to college. He would come to Dayton once a month after football season ended. I would come home whenever I could get a ride. We vowed to be true to each other. I knew that wouldn't be a problem for me. I was in love forever.

The night of our going-away dinner, I wore my favorite dress. It was navy blue with a big white collar and a polka-dot bow. (I was big on bows.) With my navy high heels, I imagined I looked at least twenty instead of seventeen. Tony seemed different at dinner—quieter than usual. I thought he was sad about my leaving, which made me happy.

After dinner, we drove to the secret place we'd been parking for the past year. He took my hands in his and very gently removed the angora-wrapped ring he had given me. I loved wrapping angora around it in a color that matched my outfits. Those big men's rings wrapped in angora were a sign to the world (at least our world) that we were going steady.

Then he said what he'd been struggling to get out all evening. "I love you and I want to marry you. You are the only girl for me, and I mean for life." I couldn't breathe. I thought he was going to pull out an engagement ring. I would've gladly accepted it, but it would have to be a secret. My parents would never allow me to get engaged at this age. We had talked about our future home. We'd even named our babies, and there would be lots of them. We had carved our initials in a tree on the corner of Jefferson and Monroe streets. We'd take our children there someday and show them the bench where we had sat for hours, talking and planning.

Then, instead of offering me a different ring, he broke my heart wide open. He put his ring in the glove compartment and said, "I want to break up with you for my senior year. I want to date other girls and go to parties. I want my last year of high school to be fun. After that, we'll get back together. I hope you understand."

I sat there in a state of shock. He kissed me and held me. I waited for him to say, "I was just joking. I don't want to be with any other girl, ever." Instead, he started the car and he drove me home in silence. When he pulled up in front of 124, I jumped out of the car. I was fighting back tears, and I didn't want him to see me cry. "Goodnight," I said. He leaned across the seat and softly said, "Hey, Mare, good luck in college." And that was it.

For the next few days, I waited for the phone to ring. It didn't. My friend Susie bought me the recording of the Skeeter Davis song "The End of the World." I made her listen to my sob stories for hours while I played it: *Why does the sun go on shining? Why does the sea rush to shore? Don't they know it's the end of the world, 'cause you don't love me anymore.* Susie just handed me Kleenex and listened.

Then Aunt Sabina got sick. She was my second mother, and I adored her. She had struggled her whole life with what she called her "ticker." She had two serious heart surgeries in Hahnemann Hospital in Philadelphia. She had almost died a couple of times. But she was a fighter, and always came back.

As a little girl, I spent hours every day in her apartment. When I was older, I'd ride my bike to meet her as she walked home from work. Sometimes during her lunch break, she'd walk by the school-yard and bring me a candy bar. During the summer, she and I would walk downtown and eat lunch at Isaly's. She would say, "Toots, are you going to have your usual lime soda and hot ham sandwich?"

Aunt Sabina made me feel pretty and special in a way no one else did. When I started high school and dating, she just watched and smiled. She never imposed on my growing up. But I always knew I had unconditional love pouring out of her little apartment next door to 124 East Madison. She always said, "Mares, living alone is no fun. Wait until you get your education, but then promise me you'll find a nice boy and marry."

She made light of her stomach issues, but I could see she was in terrible pain. I would pop in every afternoon and lay down next to her in bed as she rested. This had been my spot for as long as I could remember. Aunt Sabina always had a great story to tell me. But now I was seventeen, and leaving home. I hated the thought of her being sick, especially when I couldn't be there to help. "Oh pshaw, toots. You go to college and have lots of fun. I'm a tough old bird. I'll be fine."

★ ★ ★

After four days alone in that dark, scary dormitory, I was delighted to meet all the girls pouring onto the fourth floor. My two roommates were both tall, gorgeous blondes, and they, too, were both in love with a boy back home.

We quickly formed our gang that would be together for the next few years. We were all dreadfully homesick. We missed our homes, our parents, and our nice, safe lives. All the girls in our group were smart and had been good students in high school. In 1963 it was difficult for a girl to get into the dorm at the University of Dayton. While the school had almost ten thousand students, Marycrest Hall was the first and only on-campus housing for women. They only had room for four hundred girls, so they could be highly selective about the females they accepted.

I knew I wasn't qualified for the selective category. I had only been mildly and occasionally interested in schoolwork. I would constantly tell Mom, "I hate school. I don't want to go to college."

She'd say something like, "Oh, that's fine. It will sure save Dad and me a lot of money." Digging in her purse, she'd pull out some money and dry-cleaning slips. "Could you pick up the dry cleaning? And while you're there, ask if they might have a job for you when you graduate." Mom knew I'd change my mind when I saw the women dripping sweat with their hair hanging in their faces and swollen legs.

★ ★ ★

Most of my life, I was blessed with a whole lot of luck, which made up for my lack of talent and ambition. There always seemed to be a guardian angel on my shoulder.

My brother Joe was a junior at the University of Dayton, and my brothers Bob and Pat had graduated from the University of Dayton.

But they were not my trump card. My brother Pat's tutorials were my ticket into college.

Summers were so boring. Dad never wanted me to get a real job. He would say, "Little girl, your mommy needs you to help her here at home." And of course, he was right.

Pat, our supposed future priest, had fallen out of love with Jesus and in love with girls. He also had become a fanatic about education. For some reason, he seemed to think that I had a good but wasted brain. He decided I would be his summer project—his Eliza Doolittle. He would turn me into an intellectual.

Because of my reading problem, I had learned to memorize easily. Pat had a box of one thousand vocabulary words, and he decided I would learn all of them over the summer. He also decided I would read all the classics.

The reading part was a bit of a challenge, but the vocabulary words were a breeze. When it came to the classics, I had learned to scan, pick out key words, and get the gist of the story in a hurry. I asked Pat endless questions about the characters and the moral of the story. He knew all the answers, and I learned all the stories from our endless conversations.

By the end of the summer, I had learned all one thousand words. Pat and I endlessly made up sentences using each new word. That was the fun part.

Pat had determined that I was a genius and that I would go to one of the seven sister colleges in the East. He didn't know I was much more interested in boys than books. And that interest was going fairly well. I didn't even want to go to college. I wanted to stay right in Sandusky and make babies and brownies.

Then another act of fate—or maybe I should say luck—happened. The University of Dayton decided not to use the SAT exam for entrance in 1963, but instead require only the ACT test. This test was heavily weighted toward literature and vocabulary. Thanks to Pat, my ACT scores were off the chart.

When I applied to the University of Dayton, I not only got accepted, but I was put in the advanced program.

I got a letter from the school saying, "Mary Murray, you have tested out of English 101 and English 102. You will be in an accelerated class with fifteen of your fellow freshmen who also tested as gifted. You will also be required to take twenty credit hours instead of the normal seventeen."

No one had ever called me gifted. Worst of all, I knew I was not gifted. I wasn't concerned; I would talk with my college counselor and explain everything. I would do no gifted classes and no accelerated credit hours. I knew I would be way over my head in just the normal program.

When school started, my first class was English 103. A handsome young guy who looked a little like Tab Hunter walked into the classroom. After introducing himself as our professor, he said, "You are the brightest students in the freshman class. I will put demands on you and force you to live up to that status." I broke out in a cold sweat. I thought about just packing up and going home.

"Take out a piece of paper and a pen. I want each of you to write an essay titled, 'Why I Came to College.' You have thirty minutes."

After my heart stopped beating triple speed, I thought this might be a good thing. He'd see how ill prepared I was, that I wasn't gifted. Then I could ask to be moved back to the normal classes. So I calmed down and wrote:

> *The eight of us were standing at the train depot in Sandusky, waiting for the train to arrive. My oldest brother Tom was going to Boston College, and 124 East Madison Street would never be the same.*

I went on to describe how this routine and its accompanying tears happened every September. My grand ending was something like, "So now the baby girl who waved goodbye every year was following in her brothers' and sister's footsteps."

I felt disgusted with myself when I passed the paper to the front of the room. At least I had the weekend before I had to face the music. When I told my new roommates my horror story, they just laughed and felt sorry for me.

On Tuesday, I was back in English 103, and the handsome professor walked in the room with the fifteen essays in his hand. As if he was auditioning for a Shakespearean role, he said, "This is the most appalling pile of crap I have ever read. I don't believe any of you even got into college, let alone an accelerated class. One by one, he handed each student his or her essay. As he plunked it on their desk, he said dramatically, "Mr. Davis, F; Miss Hornbach, F; Miss Fuller, D." Finally he stopped his litany of names and poor marks, holding one remaining paper. "I will read the essay written by the only person who belongs in this class. Miss Murray, congratulations on this fine piece of writing."

I couldn't have been more shocked. After so many years struggling with reading and spelling, I decided to bask in the warmth of my moment of brilliance. This was the first time since I was in the eighth grade (and contemplating a life in the convent with Mary Eileen Shufflin) that I thought I might have some hidden ability after all.

I was homesick and love sick, but for the first time, I was finding school interesting. I had learned how to ensure I'd never have to read out loud. On the occasions a professor would say something like, "Mary Murray, could you read page 120 to the class?" I'd quickly say, "I'm sorry, Professor, I forgot my glasses in the dorm." I didn't wear glasses, but they didn't know that.

★ ★ ★

Best of all, I was introduced to a guy from Nebraska named Cliff Hillegass. I never met him in person, but his creation, *Cliff's Notes* (along with my brother Pat's tutorials), got me through college. Without the two of them, I would have never made it to graduation.

Reading was difficult enough, but when we were studying Chaucer, I had to read pages and pages of:

> *That lay by hem, they tolde it in his ere.*
> *Thus was the wenche and he of oon assent;*
> *And he wolde fecche a feyned mandement,*
> *And somne hem to chapitre bothe two,*
> *And pile the man, and lete the wenche go.*

Or Shakespeare:

> *Down, down I come;*
> *For Hecuba!*
> *What's Hecuba to him, or he to Hecuba,*
> *That he should weep for her? What would he do,*
> *Had he the motive and the cue for passion*
> *That I have?*

Every teacher warned us, "If any of you use *Cliff's Notes* instead of reading the assignment, you will get an automatic F."

I had always loved stories. It was stringing the words together that caused me the problem.

Snuggled up in bed with Cliff and his notes, I actually learned to love Shakespeare; I took recordings of Shakespeare's plays from the library and loved listening to his marvelous works. I even went to the Stratford Shakespeare Festival in Canada for a whole week of Shakespeare plays. And I got a few As, which up until now had been rare in my life.

My roommate Julie dubbed me "the girl with the golden mouth." She would laughingly say, "Murr can talk her way into or out of anything." What she didn't know was that I had learned to become a fairly good talker in order to cover up my lack of reading ability.

Mom always said, "When one door closes, another opens." It always did for me.

Dream Dies

It was the Friday before Thanksgiving weekend, and only five more days before I'd be home. I had been counting down the days for weeks. I knew Aunt Sabina was getting worse. Mom had mentioned colon cancer.

It was sunny and cool as I headed to my 1:00 p.m. class, the last one before the weekend. After class, I was running up the four floors to my dorm, which was my habit. (I hoped it would help me lose weight.) A girl I had seen around but didn't know was running down the steps. As she approached, I could see she was crying. She abruptly stopped and shouted hysterically. "The president was shot. They think he's dead."

When I opened the door to the fourth floor, I could hear girls crying. I headed down the hall to Marsh Sims' room where everyone was gathered around her small TV. As I walked in, I heard Walter Cronkite announce, "Father Huber has given the president the last sacrament." Then, fighting back tears, he said, "It has been confirmed. President Kennedy died at 2:00 p.m., thirty-eight minutes ago."

My heart sank. He wasn't just our president, he was one of us. I remembered the night he was elected. Dad cried, even though the results wouldn't be certified until the next day. He opened the liquor cabinet and took out his best whiskey, Chivas Regal, and toasted the Irish. He danced with Mom and sang "Happy Days Are Here Again." You would have thought he'd been elected president. And now Kennedy was dead.

I felt the same sick feeling in my stomach that I'd had five years earlier when the operator at Providence Hospital announced, "I am sorry. Mary Eileen Shufflin is dead."

I needed to hang on to what I had left to love. I grabbed my suitcase and my purse, and within thirty minutes I was heading for the Greyhound station. I got the first bus to Toledo. I would figure out how to get to Sandusky from there. I arrived home by nine o'clock, and went immediately to Aunt Sabina's apartment.

Aunt Sabina began to cry when she felt me crawl in bed next to her. I spent the next week and two days sitting on her bed, saying my farewells. We watched JFK's funeral together, and Aunt Sabina said, "I will die soon, and no one will even know I am gone, except you, toots."

When Maureen arrived home for Thanksgiving, she was wearing a diamond ring on her left finger. She was officially engaged to Mike Gergely, and they were planning an August wedding.

I asked Maureen to tell me about Tom's fiancée, whose visit I'd missed. "Oh, she's just really nice, and not at all like the southern snob Tom described. She wore shorts and a sweatshirt every day. She's easy and comfortable. And she didn't run to church every day, either." But then Maureen said, "When Dad met her, he jumped up and down, dancing around her. He even patted her on her butt. She's tall, and you know how Dad loves tall people. He said, 'Wooo, woo, woo, you are a big one.'

"I think Tom was humiliated but Ann just acted as if she saw this every day. Of course, she had come here from Iowa, where she had just spent three months working in a mental hospital. Probably a good prep for visiting 124." I agreed.

★ ★ ★

When I returned to the dorm after Thanksgiving, all the girls wanted to know if I'd seen Tony. I hadn't.

Julie Moretti had become one of my best friends. She listened to all my broken-hearted sob stories. She told me not to worry, she'd discovered how to get Tony back. She had a prayer that was 100 percent guaranteed to work. She'd do it with me for extra insurance. I had to say it six times a day for nine days, leaving a copy in church each time.

"May the Sacred Heart of Jesus be praised, honored, adored, and glorified, now and forever, Amen."

Say 6 times a day, for 9 days leaving prayer in Church.

Never known to fail.

I sat down at my desk and made fifty-four copies of the prayer. For the next nine days Julie and I went to Immaculate Conception Chapel six times each day, recited the prayer, and left a copy in a pew. "You just watch and see," Julie said confidently. "He'll call you over Christmas." I believed her.

I was delighted to be home for two weeks over the holidays. I baked Christmas cookies for John Tim. I had missed him so much when I was in Dayton. I felt like he was my baby, and I hated leaving him at home without me. Mom and Dad let him do what I thought was dangerous stuff, like going to Cedar Point with just Aunt Lucille. When I questioned Mom about her apparent lack of concern for John's safety, she'd just laugh and say, "Oh dear, you don't want me to make him into a sissy, do you?"

On Christmas morning, the phone rang, and a moment later Joe yelled, "Mary, the phone is for you. It's a boy." My heart pounding, I took the phone from Joe. It was Tony. I almost started crying when I heard his voice. Julie's novena had worked.

"Merry Christmas, Mare. How're you doing?" he asked. "Could you come to my house today at two o'clock for Christmas dinner with my family?" I knew his family liked me and hoped to promote our relationship. I almost agreed eagerly, then I remembered that was the same time my family was having dinner. And I'd promised to take dinner over to Aunt Sabina afterward.

Trying to sound cool, I said, "I can't come for dinner, but I'm free tonight or any other night for the next week. I'd love to see you and catch up on what you're doing."

"Sure, great. I'll call you," he said. He didn't.

MY AUNT, MY PRESIDENT, AND MY BOYFRIEND

Aunt Sabina died on December 29, and we buried her on New Year's Eve. Aunt Ann and Uncle Bob drove from Beloit to Sandusky for the funeral. Aunt Ann offered to clean out Aunt Sabina's bedroom. She took all Aunt Sabina's clothes and jewelry, her best dishes, and the hankie collection she'd promised to me. I could tell Mom was shocked by Aunt Ann's raid of the apartment, but she only said, "Sabina loved Ann. It's good that someone can use Sabina's things."

Aunt Lucille had been out of the mental hospital for a year and was living with Aunt Sabina again. I helped Mom move Aunt Lucille into to Aunt Sabina's bedroom. Soon it was almost as if Aunt Sabina had never existed. There wasn't a trace of her left.

I went back to college on January 5, my eighteenth birthday. Before I left, Dad took me into the sunroom and closed the door. Fighting back tears he said, "Your Aunt Sabina loved you more than anyone in this world. She left you the only thing she owned."

Reaching into his pocket, he took out his sister's cherished diamond ring. She had saved her pennies for years, dreaming about having a diamond ring. Dad and Mom had given her this one for her fiftieth birthday. Dad slipped the ring on my finger and reminded me, "Little girl, you were lucky to have someone love you like your Aunt Sabina did. Few people are that blessed."

Since I had started college three months ago, I'd lost my boyfriend, my president, and my Aunt Sabina—and with them a bit of my Pollyanna spirit. It was something of a relief to go back to Dayton and escape the sadness at 124 East Madison Street.

MARRIAGE DEBT

Theology classes now discussed sex on an adult level. We had known forever that it was a mortal sin to have sex outside of marriage. We would go to hell forever if we did or even intended to do "it," but didn't get around to it. But now we learned there was another sin, and it was just as mortal—only this one required us to have sex, even if we didn't want it.

Father Burns taught "Marriage and the Family," and everyone loved his course. He was a real normal, fun, and inspiring priest.

He had already covered the chapter about birth control and how you would burn forever if you tried to stop or interrupt the will of God, which would be delivered by your husband's sperm. He even said words like "premature ejaculation" and "pulling out before the act was completed." Any of these acts would thwart God's will, and of course, deserve the punishment of hell.

But then he introduced a completely new twist. He directed this to the girls in the class, and only the girls—but the boys were sitting right there, and they were all smiling big smiles.

He said, "Ladies, from the moment you say I do, you will become a partner with God in his plan for creation. You must never deny your husband sexual intercourse regardless of how often he requests it. This is called 'the marriage debt.' This would be the gravest of mortal sins." After years of raging hormones and abstinence, none of us could imagine saying "No," ever. As a matter of fact, we couldn't imagine how we could eat, sleep, go to work, or anything else if it was legal to have sex.

Then Father qualified his statement. "Now ladies, there are a few excuses for refusing. Lawful excuses for refusing are: adultery, drunkenness, insanity, non-support, or danger to an unborn baby. And ladies, of course, if you are sick. However, that does not mean, 'I have a headache.'" Everyone laughed. We had seen that in movies.

★ ★ ★

In our sophomore year, we were all taking a biology class. Unlike our high-school books, our college textbook was very graphic about the mechanics of sex. It was illustrated with pencil sketches of the male sex organ and said, "The male genitalia grows and expands when stimulated. This is called an erection. It allows the male to enter the female." That tidbit piqued our interest, to say the least. Maria Martini, who was almost engaged to her high-school sweetheart, said, "How big do you think it gets?" We all just sat there with our eyes as big as saucers.

Donna Moorehouse tapped her finger on her temple and said, "Hmmm. Well, aah, let's see." Donna always did this when she knew the answer but didn't want to act like a smarty-pants. "The book said that based on an Italian study—13 centimeters long. That, I believe, is about five inches, give or take a *weeee* bit. And according to another study, circumference was 12.63 centimeters, or about 4.9 inches."

Julie Moretti, who was majoring in home economics, jumped up and went to her sewing box for her tape measure. We started measuring everything in sight. Someone found a flashlight and we checked it. Way too big. We breathed a collective "Thank God."

Maureen Marries

In the summer of 1964, I had a job at Cedar Point, the best place on earth for a kid to work. I was selling tickets on the Cedar Point and Lake Erie Railroad. I was given an old-fashioned long skirt to wear to work. This uniform emphasized my waist and breasts while covering up my legs and butt. What could be more perfect?

I had almost four full months at 124 East Madison Street. I was sure that was enough time for me to get the Italian Stallion back in my stable. Life was pretty good.

I met some fun kids during my days at Cedar Point. I even started dating a cool guy who was a junior at the University of Michigan and drove a sports car. His Dad was a doctor in Ann Arbor, and he was clearly in the "about to be successful" category. He was nice enough, but I was already in love. No matter how hard I tried, I couldn't get interested in him. Every time we went out, I dreamed Tony would see me with him and come running back.

I was so excited. Since I was a little girl, I had dreamed about my brothers and sister getting married. I loved weddings and babies. Now there would be two weddings this summer. Mike and Maureen, August 1, and Tom and Ann, August 21.

Maureen liked me now, and we hung out together like best friends, talking and laughing. This summer was filled with wedding planning, which I loved. Mom and Maureen were delighted to turn the wedding organization over to me. They didn't enjoy planning showers, wrapping gifts, and picking out dresses the way I did.

★ ★ ★

The doorbell was ringing constantly. Maureen was getting married in two weeks and several gifts arrived daily. On Friday afternoon, John noticed a new etiquette book sitting on the hall table. There was a card saying "Best Wishes to the Bride," but no signature.

Mom began to worry. Who should be thanked for the gift? The mystery and the drama began. First, how did it get on the table in the hall? Did someone leave it at the front door? Did one of the kids bring it in?

The older boys were all working, so they couldn't be questioned.

The mystery continued until Dad got home. As always, Dad immediately knew the answer. "That son of a bitch Griffey left it. He's trying to insult me by suggesting I don't have proper manners. Peggy, I knew we shouldn't have invited him to this wedding. I should call him on Monday and tell him he's not welcome. That horse's ass."

Dad had an ongoing battle with Mr. Griffey. He had served on boards with him and they had always clashed. And worst sin of all, Henry was a Republican. Dad had had a previous patch-up-the-rift meeting with Henry Griffey. He called him and said, "This cold war between us is crazy. I'd like to invite you to have lunch with me at the Yacht Club and bury the hatchet."

When Dad came home for dinner that evening, Mom said, "Well, how did your luncheon go?"

Dad said, "Well, it was okay. Before we began to talk, I said, 'I always believe in speaking the truth. So before we order, Henry, I want to tell you, you are the dumbest son of a bitch I have met in my life.'" Not exactly the perfect start of détente.

Dad's certainty of Griffey's aggression went on and on and on throughout the weekend. "The first thing Monday morning, I'm going to take that damn etiquette book into the bank and slam it down on his desk. I'll give him a piece of my mind. He'll regret insulting me."

Pat worked all that weekend at The Town Tavern, and on Sunday morning he drove down to Crestline, Ohio, to visit his fiancée, the beautiful and refined Louise Pittenger. He arrived home for Sunday dinner, and when we were all seated, waiting for Mom to carve the roast beef, Pat nonchalantly said, "Did Maureen get Louise's wedding gift? She said she left it on the hall table Friday morning. She asked me to wrap it for her, but I forgot."

On Monday afternoon, the doorbell rang, and it was Foster China delivering more wedding gifts for Maureen. The first one she opened was a place setting of her fine china pattern. The card read, "All our best wishes for a wonderful life. We look forward to celebrating your big day with you. Thank you so much for including us in your happiness. Mr. and Mrs. Henry Griffey."

For the first time in my memory, Dad was silent.

★ ★ ★

Before we knew it, it was July 31, the day before Mike and Maureen's wedding. Things were hopping at the Murray house. I was Maureen's maid of honor, and I was determined to enjoy every minute of the weekend.

My sister's fiancé was always late, and I mean *late*—sometimes by hours. So we were all a bit nervous about Mike's arrival. Suddenly, we heard commotion in front of the house, and we stepped outside. Thank God, Mike was here—three hours late, but here. He had his good friend and law school classmate with him. Maureen had told me a lot about Ron Bosrock, one of Mike's groomsmen.

"Ron is the most sophisticated person I've ever met," Maureen told me. "He's been to Europe. He was in the Marine Corps. And everyone wants him in their wedding—he's been in twenty-two. He can tell the priest the correct protocol. And he always knows the perfect gift to give, too."

So here was the famous Ron Bosrock on the steps of 124 East Madison. Trying to act sophisticated, I offered him my hand and said, "Hello, I'm Maureen's sister, Mary. I'm happy to meet you."

That's when it happened. Right there on the front step of my childhood home. This balding former marine looked at me like I'd never been looked at before. It was the first time I *knew* I was an occasion of sin. I was wearing a multicolored muumuu that fit tightly over my hated butt and thighs, and I could feel him staring at my butt as I walked up the front steps.

My knees were shaking. Like a balloon bursting in midair, I felt my childhood end. Tony Sabino began to fade away, a bittersweet part of my past, my childhood. I was an adult now, and I knew I was going to like this guy.

When they were introduced, my dad said, "Bosrock . . . Bosrock—what the hell kind of name is that?"

Ron, not even slightly intimidated, replied, "Well, Mr. Murray, it's not Irish. It's Croatian."

My dad rolled his eyes. "Another one of those Hunky people." He'd only just adjusted to the idea of Maureen marrying a Hungarian named Gergely.

Ron immediately began to flirt with me, and I felt mature and attractive. Even my butt felt better.

He told me all about the weddings he'd been in. He loved Beethoven and hosted a birthday party for the composer every year on December 16 at which he served nothing but Champagne. He painted oils in his spare time. He'd spent a summer traveling through Europe and the Soviet Union. He loved Vienna and wanted to take me there someday. I was wowed.

There were at least three things he didn't tell me that evening:

1. It wasn't just weddings he knew about. He knew everything about everything.

2. He had picked a girl at all twenty-two weddings to fall in love with for the weekend. I was number twenty-three.

3. His oil painting was by-the-numbers.

There were a few things I didn't tell him either:

1. I hated that butt that seemed to interest him to no end.

2. I was planning on marrying Tony Sabino.

3. I was only eighteen years old.

I avoided discussing age at all. I told him I was close to completing my sophomore year in college, which was close to true (at least, close enough).

Despite our little white lies, or maybe just because of our efforts to impress each other, we had fallen "in love." My sister's wedding and that fateful meeting on the steps of 124 would change both of our destinies forever.

The following summer, 1965, my brother Pat graduated from law school and married the lovely Louise Pittenger. Joe graduated from the University of Dayton and married his college sweetheart, Sandy Metzdorf. I was in my glory. There were weddings and babies nonstop at 124.

SOLDIER BOYS

The Vietnam War was suddenly changing everything. The war was all people our age were talking about. There was a draft, and that meant any young man could be called to war. The war was changing our lives and our dreams.

Ron and I were engaged in the summer of 1965, and we were planning a June 1966 wedding. We'd get married the weekend Ron graduated from law school. On July 21, we sat on the edge of our seats waiting for the president to announce whether he was going to call up the Marine reserves. If he did, the wedding was off. Ron, a marine reserve, would have to drop out of law school and go to Vietnam. Johnson called a press conference and announced he wasn't calling up the reserves. We cheered and celebrated. The wedding was a go.

I had my picture taken for the Sandusky Register. As always, I attempted to cover up my chubby cheeks with my hair and hoped I looked nineteen, my real age. We all dreamed about finding our one-and-only, our prince charming who would make our lives perfect. I was *so* proud to have found mine, and to be wearing that coveted rock on my finger, which made my future certain.

★ ★ ★

The next winter, Joe and his wife Sandy had a baby girl, Maggie. She arrived along with Joe's orders. He was going to Vietnam.

Thousands of soldiers had already been killed, and I didn't want my big brother to be part of that killing field. I begged him not to go. Dad said, "Let me call my congressman. You have a child and another on the way. I am positive I can get you a deferment." Selfishly, I said, "What about my wedding? I can't get married without you in my wedding."

"Don't worry about me," he said. "I'll be fine. I have a couple months of training here in the States. I won't leave until after your wedding. I promise."

When I was a little girl, I thought Joe's only reason for living was to protect me. I was his shadow, and he adored me. Wherever he went, I followed. One day, when I was about five, Joe asked Dad, "Could I buy Mary? I love her so much."

Dad said very seriously, "How much can you afford to pay?"

Joe said sadly, "I only have one dollar saved. Is that enough?"

Dad thought and thought, and finally said, "I'll think about it, but in the meantime, I want to see that dollar." Joe ran up to the bedroom he shared with Pat and Jim and dug deep into his drawer, where he tried to hide his few precious possessions from his criminally minded siblings. Joe proudly handed the dollar over to Dad.

Dad took the dollar and said, "The deal is done. My boy, you own your baby sister, Mary."

I was never sure why an all-wise God would have sent such a sweet, kind, and caring little person to our madhouse. No one there knew how to deal with a really nice little boy. Our five oldest siblings never called him by his given name. In all fairness, no one in our house was called by his or her given name.

But because Joe had five older siblings, he hit the nickname jackpot. Joe the Jap, Joe the Jew, Josephine, and Pee Wee Wet Bed were just a few of them. Calling Joe these names ensured his outrage. His cute little face would turn blood red, and he'd scream at the top of his lungs. Mom would grab him, covering his mouth until he almost choked to death. She'd shove him into the cold room and slam the door.

As soon as Joe would recover and was released, Jim would say,

> *Hey Joe, when we grow up:*
> *Tom is going to Harvard.*
> *I am going to Yale.*
> *Pat is going to Penn State.*
> *You are going to THE state pen.*

Joe would start to cry again, so hard that he couldn't breathe. And again, he'd be carted off to the cold room while Jim cracked his knuckles and chuckled in the background. So torture was nothing new for Joe. Growing up in our house was the best preparation he could've had for war. If the Viet Cong had captured him, he would've survived just fine; 124 East Madison Street prepared us all for navigating difficult situations.

THE LAST SLUMBER PARTY

I opened my eyes and was wrapped in the magic feeling that only being madly in love can create. Hugging myself, I said, "Mary Murray, you are the luckiest girl alive." I wanted to cherish every moment of the next few days. This is what I had dreamed about my whole life. I thought I might burst with happiness.

I was getting married in two days. The birds were chirping outside my bedroom windows and the door to the porch was wide open. The loveliest of spring breezes floated into my room. This was where I had started my life twenty years earlier.

I was so happy it almost hurt. In forty-eight hours, I was going to walk down the aisle and become Mrs. Ronald Bosrock.

I had two glorious months preparing for my wedding with Mom. We went into Cleveland at least once a week to look for my wedding dress, shop, and have lunch. Mom said, "You can spend $125.00 for your dress, but not a penny more." Of course, I fell in love with an ivory colored dress in Halle's. It cost $135.00. My skin was so fair that a pure white dress made me look like a ghost. Mom, smiling, said, "Oh well, that dress is lovely. I will ask your dad, but I don't think he will mind." That was a joke, because we all knew Mom was the keeper of the purse. Mom was the frugal one. I was Dad's baby girl, and he would give me anything.

There was no one on earth I would rather be with than my mom. She was fun and interesting and never rattled. She treated all of us wacky kids as if we were wonderful and completely normal. I wanted to make these days last forever.

But now, I had only two days left.

This day, Molly, Patricia, and I were going to the Modernaire bridal shop on Perkins Avenue. They would try on their brides-maid dresses for their final fitting.

Patricia and Molly both looked great in their dresses. Molly was petite and looked like a young Elizabeth Taylor. Patricia was tall and slim with short dark hair. She always looked smart, which she was. I was so proud these girls were my best friends.

My life was perfect. At noon, we stopped at The Town Tavern to have lunch and celebrate Patricia's birthday. The three of us had been best friends since the first grade. We were now grown up. No more lunches at Woolworth's.

We all had had our hearts broken. I suppose we had broken a few hearts ourselves. But this day, we all had our man, our knight in shining armor. And while none of us knew what awaited us, we were young enough to believe marriage would make it all perfect.

The three of us decided we should try our new grown-up status. We had always been accomplices in each other's crimes.

We would order whiskey sours to celebrate Patricia's birthday and being adults.

The girls stopped by 124 to see my wedding gifts. Mom had displayed them all on card tables set up in the sunroom. I had chafing dishes, a purple-glazed glass whiskey sour set, a whiskey dispenser, sheets and blankets, everyday dishes, an electric frying pan, Champagne and sherbet glasses, loads of vases, and ash trays. I was registered at Foster China Shop on Milan Road.

Going to Foster China to register for wedding gifts was as close as anyone in Sandusky got to becoming a debutant.

I was going to marry the man of my dreams. He was smart and handsome. He knew everything. He had traveled the world, been in the Marine Corps, and even played quarterback on a Big Ten college football team.

And he was in love with me.

He treated me like I was an intelligent adult. I didn't tell him I had doubts about my intelligence. I had successfully learned how to cover up my problem. I wanted him to think I was smart.

It didn't matter. I was smart enough. I had been Mom's shadow since I was a little girl, and I had run the kitchen at 124 for ten years. Ron was going to practice law and run for the senate. He had been mad about JFK, whom he had met when he was a member of the Young Democrats at the University of Iowa. And I would be by his side, helping him forever.

I would make babies, lots of babies. I knew I could do that without the slightest problem. He wanted five sons, and I wanted at least eight children. I would make the most wonderful babies, and my home would be filled with great food, laughter, and endless love. I never had a doubt. My life would be perfect in every way.

The evening after our rehearsal at church and the dinner at The Town Tavern, all my girlfriends from college arrived. Julie Moretti and Ann Marie Taylor, my old roommates and now my bridesmaids, were staying at 124. The other girls were staying at the Sands Motel on Milan Road, six to a room. No one had any money, including me.

My brother Pat had made a toast at dinner, saying, "Mary thinks marriage is a slumber party that never ends." Ron stood up, and raising his glass to me said, "I hope to make it no less than that." I was so proud of him.

But tonight would probably be my last slumber party for the rest of my life. I would have to grow up—but not until tomorrow.

One of my college friends, Marsha Sims, was sitting on the sofa in our living room. She turned to me and said, "Who is that funny little man pouring Champagne for everyone?"

I was shocked, but she was even more shocked when I said, "That's my dad." The girls in college had heard so many stories about my dad, they thought he was a giant.

This was my last girlfriend night forever. We laughed and told old stories. Tomorrow, the big mystery about the taboo subject would end. I would do "it." And it wouldn't even be a sin. I would be the wise woman among them.

WEDDING DAY

Mom and Dad were both fighting their emotions. Their baby girl was leaving them.

Saint Peter and Paul Church was one short block from 124 East Madison Street. I stood on the steps of the church, the place I was baptized, received First Communion, made my first confession, was confirmed, and went to daily Mass for eight years. Now I was about to be married.

The bells of the church were ringing loudly, the same bells I had heard every day at 6:30 a.m., 8:00 a.m., and noon. My brother Joe was ushering my mom and Ron's father and grandparents down the aisle while Bach's "Jesu, Joy of Man's Desiring" was being played by the organ and violin.

I could see Mrs. Shufflin sitting in her wheelchair next to her husband in the front of the church. It was the same place she sat every Sunday. I wondered if Mary Eileen had lived, would she be walking down the aisle with my bridesmaids? Or would we both be in the convent preparing to become nuns?

Then Mendelssohn's "Wedding March" began. My only sister and my best friends from grade school, high school, and college slowly started down the aisle wearing soft, powder blue dresses and big picture hats trimmed with daisies. Friends and family filled the pews, and everyone turned to see me, the bride. This was the day I had dreamed about since I was a little girl.

Dad and I were standing at the entrance of the church. I looked deeply into Dad's tearing blue eyes. We were both struggling not to cry.

I was twenty years old, and I had not graduated from college. Dad was not happy about this day. I knew, even at this moment, if I said, "Daddy, I changed my mind," that in a heartbeat, he would have cheered silently and walked down that aisle shouting, "My little girl has changed her mind. She is too young to marry. Ron is a nice boy, but Mary needs to finish school, get a job, start her life, travel, see the world—and then maybe she will decide to marry."

I didn't change my mind.

I smiled and whispered to Dad, "Any last-minute advice for your baby girl before she becomes a married woman?"

The words my beloved father said will stay with me forever: *"Use birth control."*

★ ★ ★

Our wedding day was beautiful. The afternoon reception at Plum Brook Country Club went perfectly. We served our guests the required chicken dinner. Toasts were made. We cut the wedding cake. Dad and I danced, Mom and Ron danced, and then

Ron and I danced. I threw the bouquet to the single women. Ron took the garter off my chubby thigh and tossed it to the single men.

One of Ron's friends from college and his wife chatted with us shortly before we left the party. Bill Kane was a real character and prided himself in being blunt and outrageous. He generally succeeded at being both and making everyone laugh.

He was teasing Ron about his wedding night. He secretly gave Ron the bump sign with his fist, which I guess meant something about having sex? He then turned to his beautiful blond wife, Barbara, and said, "Why don't you give Mary some advice about her wedding night." Barbara didn't laugh. She took me by the arm and led me far enough away that the men could not hear. In a very soft voice, Barbara said, "I hope you won't be disappointed. It is not all it is cracked up to be."

We said goodbye to all our guests. I hugged Colette, who had become a good friend of mine. She would soon marry Ron's brother Larry. Giggling, I said, "You're next. Hope you know more about what is supposed to go on tonight than I do." Colette whispered, "My Grandma told me not to worry. The man will show you what he likes."

I was dressed in my "going-away outfit," a green and white coatdress and the mandatory picture hat. The party was continuing in the house, but everyone came outside as we prepared to leave. Mom and Dad hugged me, again struggling to fight back their tears. Their baby girl was leaving, but this time I wouldn't return. This time it was forever.

I was a married woman. Ron and I drove to a Holiday Inn far enough away from 124 for me to feel safe entering a hotel room with a man. By midnight, I was no longer a virgin. And I was pregnant.

PART III
THE END
1966–1974

CRYSTAL BALL

The slumber party ended along with an era in America that would never be again. Life grew me up, and pretty fast. If I had been able to look into a crystal ball that June, I'm not sure I would have been as brave as I was on my wedding day. My brother Pat used to tease me, saying, "Mary is in love with love."

And he was right.

I was lucky enough to have lived in a time when I had a chance to be young, innocent, and dream simply stupid, unrealistic dreams. The mystery of life was mine to peel back like an onion.

I am glad I was naive enough to believe that if I said a prayer every day (or one thousand times), I could change life or make something happen. And sometimes it did.

I am glad I was dumb enough to think a bra, a too-tight girdle, or a straight skirt would make me attractive. And sometimes it did.

I am glad I thought there would never be a better day than the first day that Cedar Point opened.

I am glad I had puppy love, and my heart broken and repaired.

I am glad there was a time in my life when I believed marrying the man of my dreams would make everything perfect.

No one can ever take that innocent childhood from me. Those years ended, but those precious moments would be with me forever.

After 1966, things were different. Our world was spinning with change.

Women, Vietnam War veterans, and African-Americans began to stand up for themselves.

The Women's Movement was in full swing. Women were burning their bras in protest. They were determined to gain their rights and equality with men.

Young women, myself included, wore hot pants and mini skirts. Motherhood and child rearing were no longer enough. Women needed to establish themselves in the workplace, not just the home.

In 1970, when I announced I was pregnant with my second child, a girlfriend said, "I don't know if I should say congratulations or condolences."

The Vietnam War was growing, along with the number of soldiers coming home in body bags. Young people protested on college campuses, in city streets, and at the political conventions.

In May 1970, the Ohio National Guard fired sixty-seven rounds at unarmed Kent State students. Four students were killed, and nine others wounded.

The rules of living changed. There were hippies, beatniks, and flower children. "If it feels good, do it," was their motto. There was free love, nudity, and Bob Dylan. His songs "Blowin' in the Wind" and "The Times They Are a-Changin'" became anthems for the civil rights and anti-war movements. They all gathered at Woodstock, which turned into a massive drug-aided war protest.

Young men went to Canada to dodge the draft. Many that stayed home burned their draft cards and American flags.

African-Americans demanded their civil rights. They marched

in the streets led by their non-violence leader, Dr. Martin Luther King. They demanded equal housing, jobs, and education.

April 1968, Martin Luther King was assassinated. One hundred cities were set on fire in protest.

June 1968, Bobby Kennedy was assassinated.

My life changed too. Perfect was not the "happily ever after" I had dreamed about.

December 1966, six months after I was married, we received the dreaded telegram saying Joe had suffered a serious head injury in Vietnam. He had been evacuated to a hospital in Japan.

March 1968, while celebrating my baby Matt's first birthday with Mom and Dad at 124, I was rushed to Providence Hospital. After emergency surgery to remove my gallbladder followed by a life-threatening blood clot in my leg, I spent the next two months on my back, struggling to save my life and limb.

One year later, in 1969, we almost lost Matt to a strange, unnamed sickness. Now I learned what real prayer was about.

By 1973, Joe, Matt, and I were all a bit damaged, but alive. And Ron and I had a second son, Steve.

The doctor who saved my life and my leg issued an ultimatum. Bert Seligman waved his long, skinny finger in my face and said, "You listen to me. You know I love you. You are like a daughter to me. Promise me you will never ever have another baby. And I don't want to hear any of that Catholic crap. If you want to see those two little boys grow up to be men, you will do what I tell you."

Doctor Seligman continued in an equally serious tone, "And you must do two other things. In order to save that leg, you must never gain weight, not one pound. Do you hear me? Not one pound. And starting today, you need to walk three miles every day, 365 days a year. If you do these things, you may live a normal life span and with both legs."

That day my old dreams died. I could no longer make babies or brownies.

A new and different life was ahead of me.

Ron and I had made a commitment, for better or for worse, for richer or for poorer, until death do us part. No matter how difficult life would get, neither of us could imagine not honoring those promises.

I knew my life would be with Ron and it would be wonderful. I never had a doubt.

DAD FINDS PARADISE

Florida had been paradise for Dad since he was a young man. He loved to golf, but even more, he loved the horse races. Miami had both, and after the Cubans arrived in 1959, Dad had found his soul city.

"Those hard-working, clever people are just like the Irish," Dad would say. "We Irish were driven out of our country, too. We survived because we knew how to work hard." Dad told endless stories about Cuban doctors who were now doormen or waiters in Miami. He loved their spirit. If you worked hard, Dad would forgive you almost anything. Laziness was the most mortal of all sins in Dad's book.

In 1971, Dad and Mom bought a condominium in Key Biscayne and Dad was preparing to spend his winters in Florida. For the first time since the first nine months of their marriage, Dad and Mom were finally out from under children, except John, who was in college.

In 1973, Mom and Dad invited me to visit for a week. Dad

picked my two little boys and me up at the Miami Airport. He looked tan and healthy. He was wearing Bermuda shorts and driving a used Mercedes he had bought on the cheap. But most of all, he looked happier than I'd ever seen him. He took our bags and stashed them in the trunk. "Little girl, how do you like this car? Your dad is going to be driving you in style this visit."

The two boys hopped in the backseat, and I was glad that, for the moment at least, they were quiet.

Dad thought modern-day children, including his grandchildren, were all spoiled. He'd look over his glasses and say, "That damn Spock won. This generation is rearing a bunch of self-centered, ill-behaved children."

Occasionally one of his daughters-in-law (his daughters knew better) would say to a misbehaving grandchild, "Do you want a time out?"

Dad, disgusted, would say, "What the hell do you mean, a 'time out'? That kid isn't playing football. He's acting like a spoiled brat. Time out my ass, crack his little butt."

Dad was delighted that our confirmed bachelor brother, Jim, had fallen in love with an English woman who was a Pan Am stewardess. She was lovely and refined. When Jim brought her home, Dad was sitting in the living room reading his paper. Jim interrupted, "Dad, I would like you to meet my friend from Chicago, Shirley Knowles." Shirley said she was happy to meet Dad and was anxious to meet all the family. Dad, glaring over his glasses, said, "Now, tell me dear, if you are from Chicago, where did you pick up that affected accent?"

Dad, as he drove, started to talk about Bob, his second son. Bob was now a hopeless alcoholic. "Mare, Bob is as bad as ever. He's an alcoholic. I've made up my mind. I'll support him and love him until he dies. He can live at home and Mommy and I will take care of him. Poor Bob, he just couldn't lick it."

I was stunned. Dad never gave up. He believed every human being could overcome any problem. Some may need a kick in the ass to get there. But no one and nothing was hopeless. God only knows how many kicks in the ass he'd given Bob.

Bob had always been a problem. He was born one year and four months after Tom, who'd had it all. Tom was smart and athletic, and life and learning were easy for him.

My siblings had called Bob Four Eyes and Pig Head, and he'd shared the nickname Pee Wee Wet Bed with Joe. He'd struggled with his class work in school. The nuns hated him, and he hated them.

Mom would fondly say, "Bob entered the world feet first. He was the most beautiful baby anyone had ever seen. He had big, mesmerizing blue eyes and a mass of curly blond hair. He was so long, I thought for sure he would be a basketball player. Doctor Killoran handed him to me and said, 'This little guy didn't want to stay here with us. It was at least a full minute before he breathed. But we changed his mind. He just needed a little convincing. He is a lovely, healthy boy.'"

That ride to Key Biscayne was an introduction to my new dad.

We arrived at the condo on Ocean Lane Drive and Mom was waiting at the door as the boys ran down the hall and into her arms.

As soon as hugs were over, they headed out to the balcony where they could look over the treetops and see elephants and giraffes and hear the lions roaring. The little Crandon Park Zoo was about a five-minute walk down the beach. At night, the sounds of the lions roaring made you think you were sleeping in a jungle.

I had to hide Steve's diapers from Dad. He was a madman about children being "housebroken," and Stevie was not the least bit interested in toilet training. Concerned about how his bed-wetting may have affected Bob, I was determined not to make an issue out of it with my son.

Dad was full of stories. Maureen had just left the day before with her three children. Dad was delighted with himself. He said, "You know Ennie. She is like popcorn—pop, pop, pop. But I cornered her. I bought a quart of ice cream every day and Ennie ate at least a bowl or two. She arrived at 126 pounds and left at 128.

We put two pounds on her." We always kept a scale in the corner of the kitchen so weight was easy to monitor.

The only thing that concerned me was Dad's cough. He had gotten a chest cold shortly before he and Mom had headed down to Florida. He just couldn't seem to kick it. He was annoyed by it, but didn't seem concerned.

"Little girl, come here. I want to show you something. Look at my feet. I have a nasty rash that won't go away. I think this cough is an allergy of some kind. I talked with my doctor at the Cleveland Clinic. It has been over ten years since my surgery. He didn't seem alarmed. He said coughing up blood after a cold is normal for someone with one lung. The stump from the missing lung can get irritated."

I did all I could do not to gasp when I heard the dreaded word *blood*. Mom saw my face and gave me a look that pleaded, "Please don't. Just let him enjoy his time here."

"I'm glad you're here, Marzie," Dad said. "Doctor Handwerker is a swell guy. He practices right here in the village. He has ordered a battery of tests, just as a precaution. You can drive me to Mercy Hospital tomorrow and stay with Mommy until I finish my tests. Crazy that I have to stay in the hospital at all, but fortunately it's only for one night." Dad hated hospitals.

I drove Dad to the hospital the next morning in his beloved Mercedes. He had played eighteen holes of golf the day before and swam a half hour in the pool. He insisted, "No man of sixty-five with a serious problem could do all that in one day, and it didn't even tire me out."

I tried to dig deep into my soul and get to my "Dad said it, so it has to be true" spirit, but this time it was tough.

When I picked Dad up at the hospital the next day he was like a caged lion. He couldn't get out of there fast enough.

On the way home, he said, "When you and the boys leave, I

think I'll take Mommy and fly to Arizona. We both loved Arizona when we were young. It'll give me a chance to see if there is something I am allergic to in this area. See if I can kick this cough."

★ ★ ★

I wanted a happily-ever-after fairytale, just one more time.

The next day as Dad headed to the golf course, he said to Mom, "Peggy, let's go to Hialeah tomorrow. Fat Boy is running. He's a long shot, but I have a hunch about him. Mary can take the boys to the beach and pool. We'll be home before dinner."

After lunch, I put Stevie down for a nap. Mom said, "Take an hour off and go shopping. Matt and I will read books or play cards." Matt adored his Grandma Murray, and loved to have her all to himself. I headed into the village to enjoy my precious hour of freedom.

I popped into a dress shop to try on a few cute pantsuits that were the rage. As I put my foot into a leg of one of the pantsuits, I felt a bolt of lightning hit me. The blood completely left my head and my heart began to race. I sat down on the chair. I thought I was going to faint. The clerk poked her head in and when she saw me said, "Honey, are you okay? Should I call someone to help you?"

I said, "No, I just need to get back home." I handed her the armful of clothes and got into my own as fast as I could. In a panic, I ran for the next ten minutes until I saw the condo. I didn't know what I was going to find, but I knew something terrible had happened. I prayed, "Please God, let my little boys be okay." I had nightmares about them going over that balcony, especially Matthew, who was always a climber and a daredevil.

As I walked in the door, there was dead silence. I headed for the kitchen where Mom was sitting next to the phone.

Fighting back tears she said, "Doctor Handwerker called. He

said he wanted Dad to come to his office tonight after he closes at six o'clock. He said 'Mrs. Murray, you'd better come with him. I do not have good news.'"

Mom knew, and I knew. Our hope died at that moment. We braced ourselves for what was coming.

After they returned from the doctor's office, Mom tried to get Dad to eat dinner. Dad wasn't hungry. He just sat in his green corduroy rocker and sipped a glass of red wine.

I got the boys in bed and prayed they'd be quiet and not disturb Dad.

Baby Stevie, who was always the perfect child, had been struggling with a cold. He woke up during the night tugging at his ear and crying. I swooped him up in a hurry and carried him into the living room. I sat on the rocker hoping to get him back to sleep.

When I turned the rocker, I noticed Dad standing on the balcony in his shorty pajamas. He had a glass of red wine in his hand and an empty bottle sat on the table. I never saw Dad drink too much, but tonight was different.

Steve was not yet two, but he was a big guy. I carried him out to the porch and sat down on a chair near Dad. "I'm sorry, Dad. Did we wake you? Stevie has a nasty head cold and I'm afraid he might have an ear infection."

"No, little girl. You didn't wake me. I don't feel like sleeping tonight." Dad's steel-blue eyes filled with tears. "I was just standing here looking at this beautiful world."

Dad had bought this condo before it was built because he imagined how spectacular the view would be. He wasn't disappointed. The view spanned the ocean, the skyline of Miami Beach, Miami, and ended with Biscayne Bay. It took your breath away.

We sat in silence for a few minutes. Then Dad turned to me and said, "I was just thinking about dying. If heaven is half this beautiful, I won't mind going." Then Dad kissed me good night.

The next morning, he and Mom packed up and flew back to Sandusky. Dad would begin his treatment.

★ ★ ★

We tried to maintain hope. Dad received chemo and it shrunk the tumor. Mom said novenas and Aunt Sis sent Dad relics of saints' bones to wear or carry in his pocket. Dad loved life, and he was not a quitter. Every time there was a glimmer of hope, Dad would say, "I am going to lick this damn thing. Tom Murray isn't done yet."

But the tumor came back and grew faster. We called doctors and quacks all over the country and as far away as Mexico. There was a drug called Laetrile that wasn't approved by the FDA, but promised a cure for cancer. Someone told Maureen that there was a doctor who attracted many Americans to come to Mexico for his Laetrile cure. Business was so brisk he had to construct a new clinic to treat his patients. Maureen was sure this would be the miracle treatment that would work.

Dad decided to call the doctor in Mexico. After their conversation, he talked with his doctor at the Cleveland Clinic. "Tom, I'm sorry," his doctor said, "there are endless charlatans with promises of cures for hopeless cancers. Try to make the best of the time you have left." Dad's last small hope was dashed.

In the end, Dad had one lung, and that lung had cancer. There would be no cure.

CHRISTMAS 1973

The chemo was over. The radiation was over. There were no more treatments available. Mom and Aunt Sis still hoped for a miracle, but even their faith was waning.

Christmas was sad. I tried to have a nice time with my husband and little boys, but I couldn't stop thinking about Dad. I'd wake up every morning with a sick feeling in my stomach. Then I would remember why. I was slowly losing my dad, and this time I couldn't make it stop.

Mom didn't put up a Christmas tree. She was Dad's full-time caregiver, and that kept her very busy. She acted like she enjoyed it. "It's the first time since we were married that I have him all to myself," she told me. After almost forty years, she still loved that crazy guy.

Ron and I decided to take Christmas dinner to Sandusky. After Santa Claus arrived at our house in Grosse Ile, each boy took a toy, and we got in the car and drove two hours to 124 East Madison.

When we arrived, shortly before noon, Dad was taking a nap

on the sofa.

Father Loefler, the parish priest, had seen Mom at Mass and asked, "Margaret, would you like me to bring Holy Communion to Tom after the 11:00 Mass?" She was too shy to ask, but she was elated when Father offered. She adored the saintly, soft-spoken Father Loefler. He was gentle and kind. He made you feel like he really was walking in God's shoes.

Mom was delighted to see us, but she was very busy preparing for Father's visit. Mom was always prepared for a priest to come to the house in case of a sudden or near death. As crazy as our lives were, none of us had needed to receive the Last Sacrament. This was the first time Mom was able to use the Extreme Unction equipment she had stored in the hall cupboard for as long as I could remember.

There was a definite protocol for a priest bringing the Blessed Sacrament to your home and Mom knew every step. She must have learned it at Lourdes Academy.

She took the crucifix that was over a foot long and three inches deep out of the hall cupboard. It had all the preparation materials needed. The crucifix's top slid off, and inside were two blessed candles, a small bottle of holy water, and several cotton balls.

Mom got a white linen cloth and a bowl of water for the priest to wash his hands. She placed another linen towel on the table next to Dad. It looked like a small altar.

When she saw Father's car pull up in front of the house, she lit one of the candles and met him at the door.

Mom bowed her head as she led Father into the living room. I was sitting on a chair next to the little altar. Ron had trapped the kids in the sunroom with their new toys and loads of candy so there would be no noise. It was a very solemn setting.

Dad's eyes were closed, but I couldn't tell if he was awake or asleep. Father came in very quietly and placed the small gold box that carried the host on the linen cloth. He gently bent over Dad and, making the sign of the cross on his forehead, whispered, "Merry Christmas, Tom."

Dad's head sprung up like a jack-in-the-box. His big blue eyes were raging. He shouted, "Merry Christmas, Merry Christmas, son of a bitch! What's wrong with your thinking? Can't you see I'm dying? What the hell would possess you to wish a dying man Merry Christmas?"

Poor Mom, looking mortified, just stood there holding the tiny candle. She had lived with Dad long enough to know he wasn't about to leave this world quietly.

FAREWELL MY PROTECTOR

April 17, 1974, was a beautiful spring day. The trees on Grosse Ile, where I now lived with my husband and two boys, were all blooming. The magic of spring had finally arrived. But the great exhilaration I usually felt at this time of the year was absent. I struggled to feel anything but sadness. Dad had been battling lung cancer for over a year.

I decided to drive home and surprise him with his favorite meal—lamb shanks, mashed potatoes, and apple pie. I arranged with the Connors, our neighbors who had five girls, to take my older son Matt after school. Ron would take over after that.

Stevie, almost three, sat in the front seat next to me buckled into his car seat. As always, when I turned the car motor on, Stevie fell asleep and didn't wake up until we were in Sandusky.

I had taken the same trip a few weeks earlier. At that time Dad was sitting in his bedroom in a chair next to the window, the same window where he had commandeered his world for so many years. Dad had purchased a monitor when it became difficult for him to go down the stairs. Mom had this monitor with her at all times so she could respond to anything Dad wanted. He knew I was coming, and was feeling high-spirited. He had laid out a plan.

The papers were full of news about Patricia Hearst. The granddaughter of the famous William Randolph Hearst had been kidnapped in February. By the spring, we were seeing her on videotapes saying she had become a member of the Symbionese Liberation Army, a terrorist group.

Dad's plan was that when he saw my car pull up in front of the house, he'd shout on the monitor: "Patricia Hearst has just arrived at 124. Call the police. And if that gal isn't Patricia Hearst, she's just as good-looking." Dad loved pranks and laughs, and I was delighted to see he was still like himself, so full of life.

★ ★ ★

Now two weeks had passed. Mom was shocked to see me pop into the kitchen. She almost cried with joy. She gave us both a big hug and then took Stevie into the kitchen for cookies and ice cream. She whispered to me, "I think Dad is napping. Go up and check. If he's awake, he'll be delighted to see you."

As I walked up those steps, my whole childhood flashed in front of me. As a little girl, I sat at the top of these steps every morning listening for my six siblings to leave for school. After I heard the last bang of the front door, I would yell, "Mother Dearie, come and dress me." Mom was deaf but she always seemed to appear anyway.

As I passed each bedroom, I could feel the pulse of a home once alive with children trying to grow up, fighting, loving, teasing— but always so alive. I heard the Wee Alert machine, the family rosary, Bob practicing his accordion. This had been a house that never slept. But today, there was a hauntingly dead silence, almost as if 124 East Madison was waiting to die, too.

I tiptoed into Mom and Dad's room. Dad was sound asleep. His oxygen tank was next to his bed, and the breathing apparatus was in his nose. His face seemed to almost have an aura of light around it. I stood silently and listened carefully to be sure Dad was still breathing.

Suddenly Dad's eyes opened so wide I thought he had seen God. "Dad, what is it? Are you okay?" I asked.

"Oh hello, little girl. My goodness, for a minute I thought you were my sister Mary. You look so much like her. I had a dream, and it was so real. It wasn't really a dream—it was a memory from my childhood and it was about this wonderful house. Isn't this house beautiful, sweetie?" Dad wasn't asking, he was telling me.

"What was your dream, Dad?" I asked.

"No no, little girl, not a dream, a true story."

The sun had just risen on a summer morning. I was eleven years old and had begun my first real job, delivering newspapers. Emmett, always the generous big brother, loaned me his bike for the job. I felt so grown up as I rode his big bike down to the Register. *I loaded up my papers and was thrilled to find my first deliveries would be to the richest people in the best neighborhood in Sandusky.*

The supervisor said, "Tommy, don't get used to that fancy neighborhood. Your job will be filling in for my full-time carriers while they're taking their summer vacations. You may only have this route for a week or two."

So there I was, a little guy from the west end heading up Columbus Avenue, crisscrossing Adams, Jefferson, Madison, and Monroe, and back down Wayne Street. I decided I would pretend I was rich and lived in this neighborhood and went to Saint Peter and Paul's Church and School.

Well, I was deep in my dream world, when suddenly, with a newspaper in my hand, I saw 124 East Madison Street. I just stood there and stared. I thought it was the most beautiful house I had ever seen. When I saw this house, I knew someday it would be my home. It was where my dream stopped and started.

Later that morning, when I arrived home, I heard Mom making breakfast in the kitchen for my older sisters who were heading out to work. Mom put her hand out, looking for the money I promised to bring home. I didn't notice because I was still dreaming about that house on Madison Street. Mom gave me a hug and said, "Oh my Tommy, are you daydreaming again?"

I sat down next to my sister Mary, who listened to me, unlike Gert, who always had her nose in a book. Mary, chubby and jolly, was just as smart as Gert, but a lot more fun, and she never tried to correct my stutter. She just listened patiently and always made me feel good about dreaming.

"Mary I . . . I . . . I just delivered the morning paper to the . . . the house I . . . I will live in when I grow up," I told her.

Emmett dashed into the kitchen like lightning, opening a bag of day-old donuts he'd picked up at the bakery on his way home from working the night shift. He grabbed one donut and out the door he went to his next job, shouting back to Mom, "I'll see you around four o'clock this afternoon. Today is payday. I promise tonight I'll have a little of that whiskey you like." Emmett was the best big brother in the world. He was clever and ambitious. He worked nonstop.

*Mary laughingly said, "Good for you, Tommy. I trust
there will be room for your big sister in that house on Madison
Street—and, Mama, you want to move in too, don't you?"
My mom, who seldom smiled because she was embarrassed
by her protruding teeth, said not a word, but gave me a huge
smile and touched my face ever so gently.*

Dad put his head back down on his pillow and closed his eyes.

Ever since he was diagnosed with cancer, I had never allowed
myself to cry in front of him. I remembered Dad making all my
fears disappear when he held me in his arms, which were now
bony and frail. I remembered Dad making me believe I was beautiful and smart, and could do and be anything.

On this day, I put my head down on his wasted chest. And I
wept. Dad didn't open his eyes. He just gently rubbed my hair and
said, "Don't cry, little girl. Your dad will be just fine."

I kissed him and said, "Goodbye, Daddy. I will love you
forever."

I knew this goodbye was unlike any before. This was my final
farewell to my precious protector.

★ ★ ★

Life outside of 124 hadn't stopped in deference to Dad's final
days. My oldest brother, Tom, and Murray and Murray Law Firm
were being featured Sunday night on *60 Minutes*. They were the
first law firm to use videotape in the courtroom.

Bob was now living at 124 and struggling to find his way in the
world. He was unemployed and supposedly helping Mom and Dad.
But in reality, he was mostly just drunk.

Jim, our committed bachelor brother, had married, and he and
his wife Shirley were expecting their first baby. Pat was married to

Louise, and busy growing the law firm to new heights along with rearing his two children. Maureen and Joe had each just added a baby girl to their families. John was preparing for his college graduation on Saturday, April 27. I was busy rearing my two little boys and finishing college—a promise I had made my dad.

One night, a week after my surprise visit, Dad told Mom in an amazingly strong voice, "Come over here, Peggy, and kiss me goodnight and goodbye. I am going to die tonight." For over a week, he hadn't been able to get out of the hospital bed that sat in the bedroom he and Mom had shared for over forty years—the same bedroom they had shared with each of their babies during their first year of life.

Mom pretended not to hear the goodbye part. She gently touched Dad's cheek and said, "Goodnight and God bless you, dear. Have a good sleep. I'll be in the kitchen making a coffee cake for our breakfast. The monitor is on if you need me. Get a good sleep. You'll feel much better in the morning."

Dad kissed and hugged Mom again and said with uncharacteristic calm, "Goodnight and goodbye, my love. You are and always were the best. I'll see you in heaven."

Dad closed his eyes and never opened them again.

Two days later, on April 25, Dad breathed his last breath while resting in my arms. I watched and felt his soul leave his body. For the first time in my memory, Dad was perfectly quiet.

On April 27, John Timothy Murray, Dad's eighth, last, and beloved baby boy, graduated from the University of Dayton. John missed the graduation ceremony. It was the day we buried our dad.

Thomas Murray Sr., Lawyer, Dies At 66

Thomas J. Murray Sr., 66, 124 E. Madison St., a long-time prominent Sandusky attorney and one of the founders of the Murray and Murray law firm, died Thursday at his home after an extended illness.

He was the senior partner of the father-and-sons law firm at 300 Central Ave.

A graduate of Sandusky High School, Murray studied pre-law at Notre Dame University and at Arizona Law School. He received his Juris Doctorate degree from the University of Cincinnati Law School, and earned his masters degree in law at Cleveland Marshall Law School.

He was a member of Sts. Peter and Paul Catholic Church, a member of the American and Ohio Trial Lawyers Associations, a member of the Ohio State and Erie County Bar Associations and a member of Plum Brook Country Club.

Surviving are his widow, the former Margaret Cummings; two daughters, Mrs. Michael (Maureen) Gergely, Kalamazoo, Mich., and Mrs. Ronald (Mary) Bosrock, Grosse Ile, Mich.; six sons, Thomas J. Jr., James T. and Patrick Murray, all attor-

THOMAS MURRAY SR.
... died this morning.

Thomas J. Murray

July 11, 1907 – April 25, 1974

MEMORIES OF
124 EAST MADISON STREET

I treasure all the FUN times I've shared with Mary, my FOR-
EVER FRIEND, at 124 East Madison! We are at our "silliest"
when we are together, and have been since we were six years old.
I remember kissing our boyfriends from the sunroom windows
at slumber parties, dropping her little brother Timmy down the
laundry chute, going to Mass with our PJs hidden under our rain-
coats and a Kleenex bobby pinned on our head, eating fudge in
the school lavatory, preparing "dance books" with secret messages,
("Did your dress pass inspection?" and "Remember to leave room
for your guardian angels when dancing!") In order to protect my
reputation, I can say no more—but I will cherish the memories
we've shared for a lifetime!

~ Paulette Benkey Krantz ~

Mare, I forgive you for stealing all my clothes and returning them
with spaghetti stains. Thanks for helping me get cheerleading. I
am sorry I lied to you about the Q-tip box. Mortal sin on my soul.

~ Maureen Murray Gergely ~

My dad, Ralph Windisch, always said that Tom Murray was the most honest person in town. He treated everyone equally, and if you didn't have money to pay, he'd take produce from your garden or a nice loaf of bread.

When I was in high school, Mary, his second daughter, always told me, "Don't worry if we get into trouble—my dad will get us out."

~ Barb Windisch Krause ~

My first memory of Dad and Mom was in their living room at 124, where a redecorating campaign was underway. Tons of wallpaper and fabric books were spread out in front of Mom on the French Provincial cocktail table. "Here Peggy," Dad said, "we'll take this, and this, and this!"

"Well, Tom, if you think so," Mom said, just a little hesitantly. So, Old T.J. style, BAM! The new look was decided in less than ten minutes!

~ Louise Pittenger Murray ~

I loved going home to 124 with Mary. I loved her family and being with all of them. Her mother was the sweetest woman, and the best cook. My first dinner there was very intimidating. Her dad asked me several intellectual questions, and somehow I answered them to his satisfaction. After that, I felt comfortable, and learned so much from the conversations.

We always called Mary "the girl with the golden mouth." She could talk her way out of any situation—like the time we snuck into Cedar Point before it was open and got caught. She talked security into taking us on a tour. I will always love my dear friend, Mare.

~ Judy Dattilo Stelzer ~

The best part of growing up Catholic was being able to sneak several glasses of communion wine before and after serving Mass. The worst part was that the nuns had eyes in the back of their heads. Every night after school, my buddy and I got perfectly stationed under the fire escape waiting for the girls to come out and clap the erasers. One night, we were in our glory looking up their dresses when Sister Damien attacked us. Pulling us by the ear, she shouted, "You bold, brassy boys will go straight to hell."

~ Jim Murray ~

My first memory of Mary's family home was when I came for her wedding. I remember how large the house looked, like a palace to me. I was impressed and intimidated. It seemed like everyone in her family was a lawyer.

And then there was Mary, with her bright blue eyes, wearing a lovely blue dress, all glowing and bubbly. At that time I didn't know how close we would become.

~ Colette Vincentini Bosrock ~

Being one of the poor little Center Street kids in the fifties, it was great to be Mary Murray's friend. Almost every Saturday, cousin Bev and I walked to the Murray House to see Mary. Her dear father gave each of us a quarter to buy an ice cream treat at Fisher Drug Store. The fun we had and the delicious ice cream gave me wonderful memories to last a lifetime.

~ Jean Christiansen Mees ~

Uncle Tom was a wonderful uncle. I remember when he was dying, a good friend who was a minister said, "Oh Tom, you must be so happy to be nearing eternity." Uncle Tom responded, "Tell me one person who is glad to be dying."

~ Elaine Murray Drage ~

I am truly sorry that I screamed out laughing when you were modeling for LaSalle's and they announced, "Mary Murray will be modeling a dress from our new Chubbette collection." What a relief. I have carried this guilt my whole life and now I can go to the confessional with a free conscience.

~ Ann Smith Summers ~

Mary was my roommate at the University of Dayton. She provided lots of laughs—then and now. At our Marycrest dorm reunions, my jaws always ache from laughing. I called her mom "Ma Murray." Below is Ma Murray's Sunday Coffee Cake recipe, which I've treasured for fifty years.

Sift together twice:

½ cup sugar

½ tsp. salt 1-cup flour

½ tsp. cinnamon 1 tsp. baking powder Add:

½ cup milk

1 beaten egg

4 TBL melted butter

Spread this thin batter in 8 x 8 pan, sprinkle thickly with cinnamon and sugar mixture and bake at 400 about 25 minutes.

~ Mary Ann Tayloe Love ~

The first time we drove from the University of Dayton to 124 East Madison Street was in Joe's convertible. Mary had sweet talked Joe into letting her borrow his car. There I was in the back seat, top down, barely able to breathe or hold up my head while "lead foot" Mary cruised down the highway going at least 80 mph! When we got to the house I was grateful that my vision was not impaired. And what a beautiful house—the house I had always wanted. Front and back stairs, and lots of features—like a sink in one of the bedrooms, and a kitchen table surrounded by one of the biggest corner benches I'd seen.

When I went back for Mary's wedding, the house reminded me of the house in the movie *The Philadelphia Story*. Mary's wedding gifts were displayed in the dining room and on the connecting porch. And (this made a big impression on me) her good flatware was gold! As far as I was concerned, I was in fairyland.

Mary's mom was so sweet and loving, and TJ was bigger than life, with a heart of pure gold. To this day I can still name all eight Murray kids in birth order. There are people you meet in life you will never forget, and Mary Murray Bosrock is one of those people for me.

~ *Diane Delahunty Clark* ~

Father was a magician at making things disappear. I recall one occasion when a business colleague, looking dazed and confused, asked him what happened to Uncle Emmett's building where Father had permitted him to store his restaurant equipment.

"Tom," he asked, "What happened to the house where you let me store my equipment? It has disappeared."

Father replied, "Are you nuts? Buildings don't disappear."

As it turned out, Emmett had decided to demolish the building. Emmett had assumed the tables and chairs and other accouterments found in the building were junk. He had given them to the demolishers as partial payment for their work.

That is how Father made restaurant equipment disappear without a trace.

When Emmett was made aware of his mistake, he pulled out a check, signed it, and handing it to dad's friend said, "Fill in the amount that will cover the loss of your junk."

~ Tom Murray Jr. ~

I remember dancing in the middle of the street in our baby doll pajamas at three in the morning during a slumber party. We thought we were being so wild. Then my father would pick me up and drive all fifteen girls home in his 1957 Studebaker.

~ Judy Leser Sartor ~

I am glad it really wasn't "the end of the world" when we had our hearts broken all those years ago. We were both lucky to marry our true loves and best friends forever.

~ Peggy Kautz Armstrong ~

I dubbed Mary "Mare the Bare" because she always ran around the house barefoot and in her shorty pajamas.

Mary always had a boyfriend, and she was extremely loyal to each and everyone. This provided me with endless opportunities to tease my little sister.

~ Pat Murray ~

My dearest friend:

I will always remember your slumber parties. We all wore muumuus and concocted up something crazy and fun to do. I especially loved your long telephone cord that just made it into your pantry for all those private phone calls!

~ Bev Opper Savage ~

Mary was one of my first and best friends. We started first grade together with Sister Mary Lorraine at St. Pete's in 1951, and over the last sixty-two years we have shared so many things. We laughed together over silly things, and shared our loves and heartbreaks, marriages, births and deaths. May the saga continue.

~ Rosemary Smith Hiss ~

As three young ladies (Mary from Sandusky, Karen from Defiance, and me from Fremont) arrived in Marycrest Hall, Room 409 at the University of Dayton, we were excited to begin our college days. But as it turned out, all three of us were dreadfully homesick. Upon the departure of our parents, we walked around the fourth floor at Marycrest Hall trying to become acquainted with the other coeds. It was quite evident that almost all of the girls were smoking. That was a shock to us small-town Ohio girls. We immediately made a solemn promise to each other to never smoke. Well, before the night was over, we had each purchased a pack of cigarettes. We not only smoked—we sat in our room puffing, crying, and looking at Mary's youngest brother John Timothy's picture, which was so darn cute. For some reason, he seemed to make us feel better.

It turned into a fourth floor survival ritual. Anyone who was homesick, lovesick, or had flunked a test dropped into 409 to puff and laugh at John Timmy's picture.

~ Barb Gabel Denman ~

~John Timothy Murray ~

Growing up as the youngest of eight at 124 East Madison was simply amazing.

I grew up thinking it was normal:

- For your father to shoot pigeons off the building next door, and for the neighbor to eat them;

- To not talk to your next door neighbor to the west because your brothers had picked on their kid twenty years earlier;

- To be thrown down the laundry chute;

- For a sister to constantly clean my eyes and ears;

- To have a moveable floorboard in the attic where your brothers hid cigarettes and dirty magazines (thank you, thank you, thank you brothers);

- To only go to movies that had been approved by the Catholic Chronicle;

- To have an Aunt Lucille living next door, and to only learn after childhood that she'd had a frontal lobotomy; (She told me bizarre tales and no one ever told me she was a little off.)

- To have each brother polish off a half gallon of Otto's ice cream in one sitting with peanuts and Hershey's chocolate syrup;

- To eat four cube steaks on Michael's Bakery Parker House rolls and four Federson Bakery's jelly donuts while Mom encouraged me to eat more!

It's amazing I survived, let alone turned out so normal, smart, good looking, charming, and humble.

~*John Timothy Murray* ~

SPECIAL THANKS TO:

Maureen Murray Gergely, my big sister, who provided endless pictures for this book. But best of all, she listened to every story a hundred times and laughed regardless of what I had written about her. At the end of every story, she'd say, "Promise me you will not only write and publish this book, but you won't change a word." I had to say, "I promise, mortal sin on my soul."

John Timmy, my baby brother. Since he was born in the middle of the story, he ended up being a bit player. Nonetheless, he supported me and encouraged me to write this book.

Susan Olson Murray, my sister-in-law, who listened and listened and told me over and over, "Creativity includes risk. Nothing new would ever be created if you had to be sure of success. Just do it!"

Paula Shufflin Lazarony, Mary Eileen's little sister, who fed me a fabulous lunch and cried with me as I struggled to read my story about her big sister.

Ann Murray and Trish Currie, my Key Biscayne pool buddies, who heard the stories way too many times, but didn't use ear plugs or drown me.

My high school and college girlfriends, who shared so many of these memories with me. There would be no book without you!

My friends Betsy Guthmann and Kathy Hyduke who patiently listened to my crazy stories and made me believe I could write this book.

My sister-in-law, Sandy Bosrock, who listened to stories for three straight days and always sells lots of books for me.

Lily Coyle, my project manager at Beaver's Pond Press. She held my hand, supported me, and gave me the permission and endless encouragement I needed—along with great advice.

Laurie Flanigan Hegge, my editor. She was not only skilled at her work, but also allowed the story to be told in my voice.

Jay Monroe who provided the fabulous design and made it fun, not work.

Beaver's Pond Press. I am grateful you are here for all writers with a dream. You helped two of mine come true.

The Loft Literary Center where I took several writing courses. Their classes and educators who not only taught me to write better but encouraged me to continue.

Tom Larson the renowned writer and memoir facilitator. I learned so much from both his book and his classes, which I took at The Loft.

Phyllis Theroux and her sidekicks, Pat Funk and Ellen Papoulako. I began to write my memoir the week I spent at her Nightwriters Retreat at the Bishop's Ranch in Healdsburg, California. I will treasure the memory of the beautiful setting along with the love and encouragement from the group of women who also dreamed about writing a memoir.